Quest for Barbel

Quest
for
Barbel

Tony _and_ Trefor
Miles   West

The Crowood Press

First published in 1991 by
The Crowood Press Ltd
Ramsbury, Marlborough
Wiltshire SN8 2HR

New edition 1999
This impression 2002

British Library Cataloguing-in-Publication Data

A catalogue record for this book is available from the British Library

ISBN 1 86126 277 9

Acknowledgements

The line-drawings are by Mick Nicholls and the cartoons in Chapter 12 by
Paul Martin.
All black-and-white photographs are by the authors apart from those
appearing on pages 7, 12, 23, 69, 76, 80, 125, 127, 142, 150, 154 and
173 which are courtesy of Mick Nicholls; pages 9, 19, 25, 27, 41, 42, 44,
58, 62, 68, 91, 95, 96, 104, 131, 139, 140, 145, 157, 158, 162, 166 and
174 which are courtesy of Ray Walton; and page 106 which is courtesy of
Martin James. All plates are by the authors except for Plate 13 which is
courtesy of Chris Shortis and Plates 4, 5, 6, 7, 8, 11, 15, 16, 18 and 23
which are courtesy of Ray Walton.

Printed and bound in Great Britain by
J. W. Arrowsmith Ltd., Bristol

Contents

Introduction

For more than twenty years the barbel has been our favourite fish, for several reasons. First, it is a resident of flowing waters, which include some of our most powerful and picturesque rivers. Brought up as we were on the streams of the Midlands, river fishing has always been our first love, and it was almost inevitable that the barbel, the most powerful of river species, would command a special place in our hearts.

Second, consistent success with barbel demands an intimacy of knowledge of their habits. Much of the fishing is close-range and visual, which has no equal for anticipation and excitement. Under these conditions, fishing has its purest, most primitive appeal – that of a battle of wits between man and a powerful adversary.

The methods used in our barbel angling are also ones from which we derive a great deal of pleasure and satisfaction. Watercraft has to be tuned to a high degree, the ability to interpret the current flows has to be developed and tackle control has to be impeccable. A big barbel is a quarry that will tolerate few mistakes. Unlike much stillwater angling, which can sometimes be a lottery, the more polished your barbel-fishing skills the more successful you will be.

Last, of course, there is the power of the fish. Every barbel, irrespective of size, fights like a tiger. Those heart-stopping lunges on the rod and the angry buzz of the clutch as line is torn from the spool, as a barbel surges away through the streamer weed, are as drugs to us, such is the heady exhilaration they provide. Catching barbel is addictive.

It will come as no surprise when we say that writing this book has been a labour of love. We have endeavoured to put across our approach to barbel fishing in as clear and concise a manner as possible, while at the same time keeping technicalities down to a minimum. As you progress through the following pages, it will become obvious that most of our barbel are sought in small to medium-sized rivers, generally clear and shallow in summer, which makes it possible to observe the behaviour of the fish. Nearly all the methods outlined have been based on our observations of the fish in its natural habitat, and for this reason we will state categorically that they will work in any river containing barbel. If your favourite river is too deep for observation to be possible, therefore, that need be no bar to consistent success with the species. Obviously, location is more a process of elimination than if you can actually see the fish, but if our methods are applied with commonsense and to a logical pattern you will regularly catch barbel. That we guarantee.

We do not intend to forgo this opportunity to thank a few very special people to whom we owe so much, and without whose advice and friendship over the years our angling lives would have been so much the poorer. We are both agreed that the one man who merits our particular thanks is Merv Wilkinson. In the early days of the Coventry Specimen Group, although we were both enthusiastic big fish anglers we were very ragged round the edges. Merv was, and certainly still is, an outstanding angler, undoubtedly one of the best all-rounders we have ever known, and much of the success we enjoy today is due in no small measure to his guidance in those formative years. The debt we both owe Merv is therefore incalculable. Thanks mate, and long may you get your string pulled.

Another Coventry Group colleague, a terrific angler, is Mick Nicholls. Mick fishes with us regularly, and many of the methods discussed in this book have been formulated with his invaluable assistance. Mick

never wants to pack up, it's always just a couple more casts in that swim over there. This boyish enthusiasm is a tremendous asset, and when the going gets tough Mick shines through, his inquiring mind forever searching for reasons why. As a friend and angling companion, Mick Nicholls is the man to set your standards by. Thanks, Mick, for your company.

Mick is also a superb artist; indeed, that is how he earns his living. We would, therefore, like to extend our special thanks to him for the line drawings that appear in this book.

We are privileged in having as friends some of the very best anglers in this

Top all-rounder Matt Hayes with a clonking Ouse barbel just under twelve pounds.

country, and one man who comes right at the top of that category is our old mate Dave Plummer of Norwich. For many years we have had a close relationship with Dave, freely sharing information on matters piscatorial, and to him we owe directly our thanks for the success we have both enjoyed on the River Wensum, a fishery to which Dave first introduced us. For many years Dave's lounge doubled up as our bedroom, and both Dave and his wife Linda never made us feel anything less than welcome. Such friends are rare, and we record here our sincere gratitude.

Other people in Norfolk to whom we owe a debt of gratitude are Mr and Mrs Shortis of Costessy, and their son Chris. During our many trips to the Wensum in recent years we have been allowed to park on Mr and Mrs Shortis's land, where our vans are safe from the attentions of the minority of mindless yobs with whom every English county seems to be plagued these days. Thanks to their generosity, we have been able to enjoy peaceful and relaxing fishing. Chris Shortis has been our eyes in Norfolk, keeping us appraised of prevailing conditions and allowing us to make decisions about the timing of our trips that would otherwise have been more hit and miss. To Chris, then, in no small way we owe some of our success. We have seen him grow into a fine young angler in the years we have known him, and would like to think that we have been responsible, at least in part, for some of that development. He is also a good photographer, as evidenced by the superb shots of his that appear in this book, for the loan of which we are very grateful.

Much of our barbel fishing enjoyment is as a result of our former membership of the Barbel Catchers Club, in particular the Midland Region, and our current involvement with the dynamic Barbel Society. The exchange of information resulting from belonging to these organizations is for the mutual good of all members and one direct benefit gained from the BCC days is the fishing on the Bristol Avon, to which we were introduced by fellow Midland Region member Mike Stevens. Mike himself caught many tremendous barbel from the river, and since those days Trefor's catches have been breathtaking. Thanks, Mike, and to the other former members of the Midland Region of the BCC.

Our particular thanks are extended to fellow Barbel Society member Ray Walton, the Royalty maestro, for allowing us to reproduce the essence of his work on the fascinating phenomenon of the extra barbule in the original release of this book. Space and the need to include a chapter on the upsurge of the Great Ouse barbel fishing means that Ray's contribution has had to be excluded from this reprint, but his work is no less valuable for that. Our apologies for the deletion, Ray, but we know you appreciate our dilemma.

In barbel-fishing circles, there is none so dedicated to the species as Fred Crouch. We have the deepest respect for Fred's opinions, although we do not always share them, and many of our meetings have been considerably enriched by lively debate with Fred over particular aspects of barbel behaviour. Throughout all the cut and thrust, though, the banter has always remained warm and amicable. Fred, we value your friendship. We would, however, say that chub do eat bloody crayfish! (Sorry – private joke.)

We must also give thanks to the many barbel anglers we have met on the banks of various rivers over the years. We enjoy the company of all of them and all have made a contribution to our total knowledge of our favourite species. We cannot speak too highly of excellent anglers of the calibre of Pete Cranstoun, Len Arbery, John Everard, Steve Harper, Chris Turnbull, Simon Lush, Pete Reading, Stef Horak, and our

Barbel expert Stef Horak with a gorgeous Stour specimen.

numerous friends from the Barbal Catchers Club and the Barbel Society, in particular the hard-working and dedicated committee, chaired by the ultra enthusiastic Steve Pope. Under the Presidency of our very dear friend Peter Stone, a man rightly regarded as a living angling legend, the Society goes from strength to strength. Special thanks also go to four young men whose skill and dedication to barbel fishing ensures that we relative old-timers are kept on our toes, and they are our good friends Stuart Morgan, Matt Hayes, Adrian Busby and Matthew Bodily. All these men are kindred spirits whose friendship we value deeply. It is our fervent hope that this feeling is mutual.

This introduction could not possibly be complete without thanking two very special ladies, Fran Miles and Kath West. Over more than thirty years, they have both endured our often long absences from home with tolerant resignation. It must have been very difficult for them at times, and we realize that we have often been selfish in our irresistible addiction to catching big fish. What more can we say than, ladies, we love you.

The same comments can be made about our children, Chris, Debbie and Jacqui

INTRODUCTION

Miles and Lisa and Lindsey West, who have been forced to endure many days when dad was not around. To our combined families, therefore, this book is gratefully dedicated.

We would like to end this introduction with two serious pleas. More than ever before, our fishing, particularly in running water, is under threat from all sorts of outside influences. It is vital that we do whatever possible to earn a reputation for being responsible human beings, who care about the environment and its wildlife. Please take all your litter home with you; it takes very little effort and preserves our fisheries for future generations. It is not clever to hide rubbish in long grass rather than go to the trouble of disposing of it properly. I am sure that when anglers do these things they do not intend a song-thrush to die a slow lingering death, tangled in nylon line, or a sheep to suffer gangrene as a result of gashing its foot on a discarded luncheon-meat can, or a cow to die in agony after swallowing a plastic bag. But these things happen. So please, think of the possible consequences and please act responsibly.

Every angler who cares about the future of his sport should be a member of the body that leads the battle against the polluters of our waterways, and that is the Anglers Conservation Association, or ACA for short. The director of this organization, Mrs Jane James, needs all the backing she can get from the general angling public to be able to fight the many costly legal actions she undertakes on our behalf. You should not even need to think twice. If you are not already a member, then join immediately by sending a cheque for £10 payable to the ACA to Jane James at the following address:

Anglers Conservation Association,
Shalford Dairy,
Aldermaston,
Reading,
Berks, RG7 4NB

There is now no more to say except to extend to you the most exciting invitation we know: come barbel fishing with us.

1 Tackle and Baits

TACKLE

This section is concerned solely with a general résumé of the equipment we consider the basic armament for our barbel fishing. More specific terminal rigs, to meet many varying circumstances, summer or winter, will be found in the relevant chapters on angling techniques.

Rods

With such a wide variety of good, reliable tackle available to the angler of the nineties, it is simply impossible to say which is the best rod for barbel fishing. It very much depends on the angler's personal preference, and the action he prefers. Fishing is, after all, primarily about enjoyment. A rod for barbel fishing must nevertheless meet certain criteria to be capable of matching the most powerful of our river species. A very light, flexible rod may be an absolute joy to use, but if every barbel you hook is lost because it is simply not up to the job the enjoyment will soon begin to fade. Conversely, a rod that is too stiff and powerful will lessen the thrill of the fight, and is also likely to cause hooks to pull out at close range, because the rod lacks the flexibility to respond to a last-minute plunge by a huge barbel.

We now use exclusively rods produced for us by Century Composites in our Pulse range. For all round work, the 11ft 3in or 12ft 3in TM Barbel and TM Big River are

the ideal choices, being of progressive through action. For the special requirements of upstream legering, the slightly faster actioned 12ft TW Upstreamer allows lightning fast pick-up of slack line, while for the raging flood, when possibly 4oz of lead is required, the TW Floodwater comes into its own. This is a real power-house of a barbel rod, certainly too strong for more normal conditions.

The Pulse range features removable tip rings, and spigoted 2oz and 3oz quiver tips, all of which are fitted with adapters to take beta lights or night lights. If your rods do not possess such adapters, beta light attachments appear on page 52.

Reels

As far as reels are concerned, if you play fish by backwinding then almost any good fixed-spool will do the job adequately. However, if, like us, you enjoy the thrill of fighting the fish off a properly set clutch, then it is obviously imperative that a reel is chosen with an efficient and reliable clutch mechanism. For many years we both used Cardinal 54 reels that never let us down, but as these are getting long in the tooth, we have switched to Shimano 4010 models that are perfect for the river angler, with a silky smooth clutch.

Line and Hooks

Tony uses Drennan Specimen Plus line, or Sufix Synergy for extra abrasion resistance,

Tony with a superb Cherwell specimen.

while Trefor favours Bass Pro Premium XL Clear, both of us using Drennan Continental boilie hooks, in which we have absolute confidence. Our old favourite heavy-grade Au Lion D'or hooks, pattern 1534, are no longer available. Like any tackle item, however, they will let you down if not properly maintained, and we change our line regularly throughout the season, and test all hooks before use. Any hooks showing any sign of rust should be discarded. For the barbel fishing we do, spools are carried loaded with 8lb and 10lb line, the heavier being chosen when we are

fishing for big fish in snaggy swims. We will concede that lighter tackle could be employed for more average-sized fish in open water, but would never drop below 6lb line for barbel fishing in any circumstances. It is not clever to leave barbel trailing lengths of light line behind them, because the angler mistakenly believes it to be more sporting to us inadequate tackle. For big baits, our standard hook is a size 4 or 6 Drennan Continental boilie hook, with a size 8 being used for particle clusters – for example, a large bunch of maggots. For fishing in true particle style, on a sunny summer afternoon or winter feeder fishing, where a smaller hook is indicated, Trefor's choice is a Drennan Super Specialist in sizes 12–16. Tony prefers black Drennan boilie hooks sizes 12 or 14 for hair rigging particles such as casters, but for feeder fishing with maggots mounted direct on the hook the choice is Drennan Super Spades in sizes 12–16. For jungle warfare with a big barbel, however, the Drennan Continental reigns supreme.

In recent seasons, we have drawn on carp fishing experience in changing to soft hooklinks, the most commonly used for big baits being Drennan Dacron, available in green, brown or black to suit various bottom compositions. Dacron is the most tangle resistant for very mobile fishing. For more static applications, excellent alternatives are Drennan Carp Silk and Rod

An immaculate 10lb 6oz Wensum fish.

Hutchinson's The Edge. The most recent innovation is very thin, high-strength braids, especially important in feeder fishing or for presenting particles in clear water where high strength is required. The one we use is Sufix Herculine, which is wonderfully limp and of very consistent quality.

Knots

A quick word about knots at this juncture will not go amiss. For attaching hooks to nylon or any of the materials mentioned, a seven turn whipping knot, as advocated for spade-end hooks but which is even more secure for eyed hooks, is extremely strong and reliable. This knot has been found to have almost 100 per cent strength and has never let us down yet. After passing the line through the eye, form a loop in the end of the line and lay it along the hook shank. Then pass the loose end round the loop seven turns, before passing the end through the loop and drawing tight. The knot is then pulled down to lie flush with the hook eye. If you prefer the more easily tied blood knot, the tucked blood is adequate for nylon, but for the softer materials a multiple tucked blood knot is far more secure.

For attaching swivels, the tucked blood will again suffice for nylon, whereas Dacron requires ideally at least three tucks. The multiple tucked blood knot is also used for the limper materials such as Carp Silk, but because of its exceptional suppleness and low diameter it is advisable to make at least three passes through the swivel eye before tying the knot itself. This prevents any chance of slipping.

An important item of equipment is a rig wallet containing at least six ready-made-up hooklinks, easily slipped into a jacket pocket, and we use the one produced by our own company Double T that markets products specially designed for the mobile river angler.

Weights

It goes without saying that all weights should be lead-free, and we carry a range of bombs from ½oz to 2oz, with some flattened for extra holding power. Exactly the same comments apply to swimfeeders, more orthodox patterns being used for summer work and the flattened varieties, which carry greater weight, for fishing in the heavier flows of winter. As well as the feeders themselves, we also carry some sledge leads for clipping on to the feeder for extra grip on the riverbed.

For barbel fishing to be at its most effective, particularly in the winter, it is important that you should be able to change the weight of your terminal rig quickly, to suit the different requirements of each individual swim you come to. For this reason, our rigs always include quick-release snap swivels, which enable leads or feeders to be changed in seconds. Ordinary swivels are invariably Berkley 50lb test.

Ancillary Equipment

The ancillary equipment is of no less importance than the main tackle items. The landing net should be adequate for the job, and we use triangular models with 36-inch arms. A recommended modification, since much of the fishing is carried out in very streamy water, is to wrap 8 inches of half-inch lead strip round the base of the mesh, to prevent it being washed away in the current. An extending handle is a must. Many stretches of some rivers – certainly the Bristol Avon, Cherwell, Severn and Dorset Stour – have high banks, which can become dangerously slippery in high water. Leaning out over floodwater with a short-handled net is not to be recommended if you are planning to see your retirement. You must always use micromesh. After catching the barbel of your dreams, you do

not want it to go back with a detached dorsal spine or a split pectoral, where the large fin has caught in coarse netting. Good micromesh is available from most tackle shops, and it is criminally irresponsible to use any other.

This brings us on to our pet hate, keepnets. They have no place whatever in barbel angling, being manifestly unsuitable for retaining these most streamlined of fish. This is not to say that we disagree with the retaining of barbel in certain circumstances. Far from it. It is often advisable, especially with a large fish that has given a long, hard fight, and if the river is flowing at all strongly, to keep the fish in a soft carp sack for as long as it takes to recover its strength and be capable of coping with the current. A few years ago, we were extremely lucky not to lose a 9lb Cherwell fish. That barbel fought tremendously hard in a strongly flowing river that was some two feet above normal level. Despite a half-hour rest in a carp sack, and being released in a gentle bankside flow, it was observed a minute or so later surfacing belly up in the main stream. Fortunately, fast shallows were about forty yards downstream and, although two wet feet were the result, the barbel was safely retrieved and put back in the sack in quiet water for a further hour, when it went back strongly. Provided there is an adequate depth of gently moving water, the carp sack is a perfectly acceptable method of retaining barbel, both for their welfare and for the occasional trophy shot. Both of us carry at least two sacks at all times.

Two of the most important items in our tackle box are the thermometer and bait dropper. Good conditions for winter barbel fishing are very much dependent on water temperature, and use of the thermometer on every trip will quickly give you much vitally important information. Similarly, consistent success with barbel depends on accurate and thoughtful feeding of the swims in which we hope to find them, and the bait dropper is a truly essential accessory. So much importance do we place on this item that we both carry at least three with us. In our opinion, loss of the bait dropper would spell the end of our efficiency as barbel anglers for the remainder of that session. Likewise, we would never embark on a night session without carrying two reliable torches, for weighing fish and retackling if necessary, with spare batteries for each. These are obvious examples of nothing being left to chance.

For the bulk of our barbel angling, as will become more apparent as you read further into this book, mobility is the key-word to our approach. Most sessions will see us cover a long stretch of water, continually commuting backwards and forwards, and for this reason holdalls, umbrellas and heavy fishing chairs are usually left in the van. The lighter you can travel, the more efficiently you can fish and the more you are inclined to move swims. There is nothing more off-putting than having to move a mountain of gear,

The business end of a double.

and this will often lead to laziness and missed opportunities. There will be occasions, obviously, which call for a more static approach, and this has particular relevance in feeder fishing. There is nothing wrong then in setting out a more comfortable stall, and the Fox adjusta level chair is just about the last word in angling comfort. The older we get, the more we appreciate such considerations.

For many years we have used a tackle-box-cum-seat so that when we move swims all we have to pick up are the box, rod and landing net. Items needed through the session, such as leads and hooklinks, are kept in our pockets, as are lightweight overtrousers and a spare scarf and gloves if it turns especially cold. These days, Tony prefers a lightweight Rod Hutchinson Ambience bib and brace that is both warm and waterproof, worn under a three-quarter length Ambience jacket. With this combination, it is no problem fishing right through a winter's night. Angling efficiency is impossible if you are wet, cold or both.

For weighing fish, we would again implore you to refrain from using coarse netting. Please equip yourself with a soft weigh-sling or, failing that and considerably cheaper, one of those large oblong plastic bags that wallpaper is sold in. Being virtually weightless, they make the weighing of specimen fish much easier. For the weighing, we both use Avons, although brass Salters are equally good. Whichever you use, go to the trouble of checking their accuracy every so often.

For our summer fishing we both carry screw-in scythe blades, for fitting into our landing-net handles, and lightweight drags, for swim creation. Neither would we be without swimming trunks and a towel. There is no quicker way of establishing the main features of a stretch of river than by wading it. No amount of work with a plummet will reveal so much information so quickly.

Lastly, a plea. You will always have room in your box or bag for a lightweight plastic dustbin liner. Please get into the habit of collecting any litter you come across on your fishery, even though you may not be responsible for it. It takes very little time and will help to divert some of the criticism being levelled at anglers. If we all acted as watchdogs for each others, we could soon clean up our act.

BAITS

There is absolutely no doubt that, in most cases, the actual hookbait used is largely irrelevant if the swim preparation work has been carried out properly. If the barbel have no reason to be afraid they will take anything that is edible. The choice of bait is, therefore, usually governed by factors other than whether the barbel will eat it, such as its resistance to small fish, its visibility, presentation possibilities, and so on.

As will quickly become apparent as you read through this book, the basic bait item in swim preparation, summer or winter, is hempseed, simmered slowly until it has split to reveal the enticing white interior. We have never come across any barbel yet that have failed to respond to mass baiting with hemp. Even if it is not being used as a hookbait, it is the most reliable free feed item you can use. Both for holding feeding fish in an area and for locating groups of barbel in a new stretch of river, it has no equal. Having said that, we now mix hemp with that superb seed mix Partiblend, available from Hinders of Swindon. Hemp is such a basic necessity for successful barbel fishing that we strongly advise that you buy in bulk. We use vast amounts of hemp.

As well as being a mass background attractor, hemp is also a terrific hookbait in its own right. It is obviously very fiddly to use on a hook, and almost impossible on the large, strong hooks almost always required in barbel fishing. There are two ways in which this problem can be overcome, and these are covered in Chapter 4.

As well as pure hemp itself, successful baits for use on large hooks can be made incorporating hemp in a variety of pastes. The simplest version would be to mix cooked hempseed with normal bread, cheese or meat pastes to make a crunchy mixture; or you can liquidize the cooked hemp and add it to the same pastes. Dry ground hemp can be mixed with naturally moist products such as liver pâté or sausage meat to produce a very effective bait. If eels are a problem, a bait that has been found to be very effective in avoiding them, and yet is one the barbel love, is liquidized cooked hemp mixed with enough milk powder and wheat gluten to form a stiff, pliable mixture. In place of the cooked hemp you can use dried ground hemp, but you will need either water or eggs to bind the mixture. As the dried hemp does not have the same attractive level of smell as the cooked variety, a recommended refinement is to include about 5ml of concentrated hemp flavour per pound of bait.

Best known barbel bait of all is luncheon meat, used in cubes straight from the tin. It can be flavoured with liquid concentrates or coated with powdered extracts or spices for enhanced attraction. There are several good varieties, our favourites being Celebrity and Tulip. As a variation from luncheon meat, bacon grill is always worth a try, and has produced many large barbel. A very useful refinement when using luncheon-meat baits, especially where they have been used extensively, is to use them in different shapes from the usual cubes. It is also worth mounting three or four little cubes on a hook rather than one big one,

11lb 12oz from the Wensum.

rather like cheese and pineapple on a cocktail stick. It looks different, and the greater surface area releases more of the attractive meaty smell into the water.

A bait that used to be much more popular twenty years ago than it is today is sausage or sausage meat. The simplest method of using sausage is simply to impale half a banger on a large hook, taking care, if skinned sausages are used, that the skin does not impede hook penetration. Alternatively, you can make a tremendous bait out of sausage meat. This is usually too tacky to be used as bought, so you need to mix it with a bulk binding agent. The simplest is very fine breadcrumbs, but you can use proprietary groundbaits, ground breakfast cereals, ground hemp, biscuit meal, or even custard powder if that takes

your fancy. They will all catch barbel. Sausage or sausage meat baits have largely been superseded by luncheon meat for today's barbel anglers, but, believe us, they are still very well worth a try. On hard-fished waters where the barbel are perhaps becoming a little spooky, their use could provide some startling results and put you one step ahead.

Cheese paste is a good old standard barbel bait. Some processed cheese or even hard cheese can be formed into usable baits on their own without addition, but, in winter, cold water often makes these baits too hard. Hook penetration is therefore uncertain. It is always better, even in summer, to use cheese in the form of paste, and one of the best recipes we know is to take an orange-sized ball of pastry and mix it with 8oz of finely grated mature Cheddar cheese and 4oz of finely grated Danish Blue. This makes a lovely soft bait with a really strong aroma. Our wives love us when we start making this one!

As well as the pastes mentioned, all of which have caught plenty of barbel for us, any paste bait that will catch carp will also catch barbel, and if you really want to delve into the bait question you can do no better than read up on your carp bait recipes.

Apart from hemp, other particle baits are very effective in barbel angling, especially in clear water conditions, and top of this particular list come sweetcorn and tares. Both are superb hookbaits, tares being particularly useful when eels are a nuisance. We have yet to catch an eel on tares. Corn is an enigma. On some rivers, the barbel will respond to any amount of corn in a swim; on others more than a modest amount spooks them. You have to learn what your particular barbel want and will tolerate. Used properly, corn is an excellent barbel bait, both as free feed and on the hook.

The most used particle baits are, of course, maggots and casters, and there is no doubt that the humble maggot is one of the most devastating baits of all. Barbel switch on to large quantities of maggots in much the same way as they do to hemp, and if they are used in sufficient amounts the fish lose much of their customary caution. Even on very hard-fished waters, maggots produce regular catches of fish. They can be used either in the traditional manner or in large bunches on a big hook. Whichever approach you adopt, maggots become more effective the greater the amount you use. The same comments apply to casters, which are a really superb barbel bait, but obviously very expensive to use in quantity. If cost is an overriding consideration, it is wise to consider all the other particle bait possibilities before progressing to a maggot

or caster campaign.

A very neglected and underrated barbel bait, and yet one we consider one of the best of the lot, is the lobworm. Lobs are the only bait that will take barbel summer or winter, in clear water or coloured, and we would never venture on to any barbel fishery without a few lobs in our tackle box. Lobworms really are a barbel bait *par excellence*, and we have lost count of the times when the humble worm has produced a fish when other offerings have either failed to arouse the interest of the barbel or been eyed with obvious suspicion. Be in no doubt that we place lobworms right at the very top of our list of effective baits, well worth the backache incurred in their collection and the problem of hot-weather storage. When a barbel comes across a nice juicy lob in the summer months, he must think that it's his birthday.

One trick that has produced a large number of barbel for us is the ploy of using cocktail baits, which has been used for years in catching big tench and, in the last year or two at Queenford, big bream. The two most used to date have been lobworm and corn or meat and corn, but several fish have been taken on maggot and corn, caster and corn, caster and maggot, and hemp paste and corn. Obviously, the list of possibilities is limitless. Cocktail baits are always worth a try when single baits have failed. One good example is when using luncheon meat in the summer during the day. Barbel will often spook at a large lump of meat, but use a small piece to garnish two grains of corn and you have an excellent bait which does not appear to scare the fish.

Coming right up to date, barbel love special pastes and boilies, but they must be educated to recognize them as food. The best way of doing this is to prebait for several days before fishing, if possible. But please do this in moderation, as the intention should not be to spoil the fishing of

The Top Stile – a famous swim on the Upper Trammels.

other anglers. Most carp recipes will catch barbel, but special barbel mixes are now available from some suppliers, including our own Action Baits, which has four well-proven barbel recipes in the range, together with complementary flavours. These special pastes and boilies are a lot like hemp in their powers of addiction. Get the barbel feeding hard on them and they will become totally preoccupied. Boilies are fished either side hooked or on a short hair.

Last but not least, we have bread in all its forms. While generally not recognized as an especially effective barbel bait, it will nevertheless take fish in clear conditions in winter when the river is showing an accept-able temperature. When meat baits are ineffective, but you still prefer a large bait instead of switching to the swimfeeder and maggots, a piece of flake or legered crust could provide an unexpected bonus.

There it is, then – a general summary of the main baits we have used to take barbel. Let us, however, repeat what we said at the start of this section. If you take the trouble to prepare the swims properly, and are then capable of approaching and fishing them without scaring the living daylights out of the fish, you will find that the actual hook-bait has very little importance. The barbel will eat everything in sight, including that mouth-watering morsel attached to your terminal rig.

19

2 Location and Swim Selection

As in all fishing, the most important aspect of success with barbel is location of the fish you wish to catch. There was never a truer statement than that you cannot catch a fish that is not there. Nevertheless, the majority of anglers pay scant attention to this most vital of tasks, usually being in far too great a hurry to start fishing. Too often, swim selection is based upon what suits the angler rather than what suits the fish. Consider this. If a man goes out to shoot wild duck, would it be sensible for him to walk blindfold across the middle of a field and fire his gun haphazardly in the air now and again, in the hope of achieving the odd lucky shot? Of course it wouldn't. Why then are most anglers content to seek their quarry in the same handicapped fashion? Obviously, it makes very little sense.

Barbel location in the early part of the season will largely revolve round the spawning process, which may occur at any time between May and late July, depending on the prevailing weather and water conditions. A cold spring will see the barbel still awaiting the annual procreation ritual on 16 June, and they will consequently still be found grouped on or near to the spawning beds. This is important not only for locating fish to catch on the day, but also for assessing the overall potential of a stretch of river, particularly if it is one you are investigating for the first time. Conversely, a warm spring may find the fish spawning as early as May, and close-season

reconnaissance of the river will prove invaluable. This was certainly the case during the spring of 1989, and, if the prediction of a succession of warmer summers to come is correct, time spent on the banks during the close season will pay handsome dividends.

While they are awaiting suitable spawning conditions, the barbel feed hard, especially the gravid females, and you have an excellent chance of catching an exceptional specimen. Remember, the fish may travel as much as two or three miles to suitable spawning areas, and the large concentration of big fish provides an excellent chance of exciting early-season action. Not long after spawning, the fish may disperse because of angling pressure, and become much more difficult to locate consistently.

While awaiting spawning, the barbel will usually be found in the nearest available cover to the spawning areas themselves. This could take the form of overhanging bushes or trees, beds of streamer or bulrushes, and cabbage patches. These may be located either upstream or downstream of the shallows, but the barbel will be as close as possible, while feeling secure. Particularly reliable are the first twenty yards of water downstream of the shallows, where the gravel cannot be seen because the water is too deep. Any area of sudden depth change will always be an attractive feature. If there is weed cover as well, this area will be a consistent bite producer.

A known barbel holding area.

At this time of the year you should not be discouraged if the only fish you see are small ones flashing over the gravel. The small males are very active before spawning, and their presence is a good indicator that the larger females are not too far away.

After spawning is complete, which is an exciting spectacle in shallow water, the barbel will remain in the vicinity of well oxygenated water for a short while, from a few days to a couple of weeks, for the purpose of cleaning themselves and using the well aerated flow to help build back their strength. This gives another opportunity for very productive fishing, as very big fish will feed avidly in water only inches deep if they are not disturbed. We have both caught many large barbel during the dark hours of a summer night from streamy

water no more than a foot deep. If you have never experienced a big barbel powering away over such shallows you are in for some explosive action.

Once the annual spawning ritual has been completed, and the fish have settled down into their normal routine, the location procedure must be started all over again, although many fish will still be found in the general proximity of the spawning sites. The first thing to realize is that small groups of fish colonize different stretches of river, and that no swims exist naturally as such. Individual fish may normally browse over quite a large area, taking up residence at different stations at different times, to take advantage of localized food supplies. What we are trying to establish first of all is the general area of

21

residence of a group of barbel. Once that has been found, the actual swim from where they can be caught will largely depend on the angler's swim preparation and baiting technique. This vital aspect is covered in depth in the next chapter. It follows from that statement that we can largely control the feeding position of the barbel in any area, which is vitally important for consistent success. Our approach invariably is to bait areas no more than a rod length out from the bank, where the water is such that we can clearly see the gravel. Not only does this obviously allow us to see the fish easily; it also permits their behaviour to be carefully monitored, in particular their reaction to our baiting. Also, of course, the closer to the bank is the fishing position, the more

delicate can be the introduction of the terminal rig. As we shall see later, this can be a critical factor. By the same token, bankside disturbance must be kept to a minimum. Fluorescent lime-green waterproofs or floral-patterned Bermuda shirts and matching shorts, both of which have been observed on the banks of the Avon, are therefore not recommended as suitable attire.

All barbel stretches will contain at least one holding area, where the fish spend much of their time when not actually feeding. For various reasons, it is often not feasible to fish this area efficiently, and a swim will be created away from this spot. But it is important that it is not too far away. For instance, there may be a fifty-yard stretch

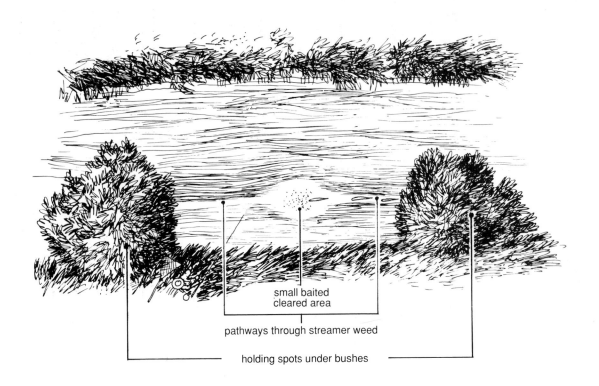

small baited
cleared area

pathways through streamer weed

holding spots under bushes

Selecting your swim.

The result of good location. Phil Smith with a superb thirteen-pounder.

of streamer weed cover over generally shallow water, but containing one substantial mid-river depression. That depression will be the holding spot, and it would be sensible to create the feeding area no more than ten or fifteen yards away, either upstream or down. The barbel will commute regularly to feed so long as they feel secure in the knowledge that they are not too far from home should danger threaten. There is little point creating a swim thirty or forty yards away from the nearest possible holding spot; that is simply inviting failure.

The streamer weed bed is obviously one of the better known features to attract barbel, but the fish will also be found in the vicinity of overhanging bushes and trees, bulrush beds, and water lilies. Again, a good ploy is to bait the nearest area of clear

gravel where observation is easy. If no such clear area adjacent to a suspected holding spot is present, then you can create one, either with a small drag or, better still, a small scythe blade, which is more selective. In all weed clearance operations to create barbel swims moderation is the keyword. You are not advised to undertake mass weed removal. That will be counterproductive and make the barbel extremely spooky. Rarely will they feed confidently over a large barren area. All you need is a small clearing just big enough to fish, but with plenty of cover surrounding it in which the fish can hide.

In fairly sparse weed you may notice natural channels through the foliage, and these act like highways for the fish. It is a simple matter to open out one of these

23

channels to create the fishing position. You will then know at exactly what point the barbel will enter the swim to feed and be able to place your bait accordingly. In very dense weed it pays to create artificial channels from the holding spot to the swim itself.

Imagine creating a clear area on a short section of open bank between two other lengths heavily overhung with alders. After making the swim itself, it would pay to construct pathways through the weed to both upstream and downstream holding spots. These should not be too wide – a few inches is ample – but they must be defined enough so that the barbel will naturally follow them when they move in and out of the new swim.

Before you select a spot for creating any new swim, we cannot stress too strongly how important it is to ascertain the surrounding riverbed geography, either by plumbing or, infinitely better, by getting in the river and wading. We are still often amazed by how many depressions in the riverbed we find by wading, depressions which are often completely undetectable visually. Really, it is all common sense. Before creating a new swim, make sure that you have chosen the most advantageous position, having taken all the factors into account. One such factor is whether the gravel contains any slopes or shelving areas. If such a feature is present, it will be a preferred feeding site. Barbel love to feed up a slope.

As well as the swims so far discussed, either natural or artificially created clearings close to cover, there are other features to look for which are equally likely to contain barbel. The first of these are sunken snags, which are almost always top-class barbel swims on every river we fish. The most obvious snag is a fallen tree, but the famous snag swim that we fished at Berrington on Severn was created by a sunken

car, while the well-known snag at Atcham was actually a riverbed wall, long since fallen into disrepair. In the same way as visible cover, sunken snags obviously give the barbel feelings of added security. The same reasoning explains why swims around bridge arches are so productive, and the famous railway pool on the Royalty is a good example of that.

Reliable as the previously mentioned swims are, it is a grave mistake to ignore other areas, since some barbel rivers have a distinct lack of any of the features so far described. In the same way as for chub, smooth glides provide consistent barbel fishing, especially if such glides are of slightly deeper water above or below rapids or turbulent shallows. If these glides contain streamer weed, so much the better, and an excellent example of a swim of this type is the Telegraphs, again on the Royalty.

Another first-class area for consistent barbel sport is the smooth glide on the run-out from a weirpool, and the gentle flow back along the side walls. In areas like these we are looking for even-paced water of continuous smooth surface; constantly boiling water is useless for barbel fishing under any circumstances. Also unproductive, in our opinion, is the white water under the weir sill, despite the many thousands of words that have been written extolling the virtues of such swims. After twenty-five years of barbel angling we are both still awaiting our first barbel bite from this area. Nevertheless, barbel fishing friends have reported odd fish from this white water, so investigate it if you wish. However, our advice would be not to waste too much valuable fishing time there. The same comments apply to dead slacks and turbulent eddies. The nature of these swims means that the riverbed is often littered with debris, which is a deterrent to barbel.

Matt Hayes creeps up to an Ouse hotspot.

Very reliable swims indeed are the channels between bulrush beds, or the gently flowing water behind rushes. Memories of Throop fisheries on the Dorset Stour in the sixties come flooding back when we find such features. Such memories are of a much younger Miles and West probing away with a consuming passion for our first double-figure barbel. If only we had known then what we know now! Rushes often divert the flow, forming a crease-type swim, and barbel will frequent this feature. If the flow happens to be diverted under good cover, then you have discovered one of the best barbel swims of all. The most consistent swims on the Cherwell are of this type. The importance of cover for the barbel to hide under cannot be overstated, and a good swim can be transformed into an excellent one by the artificial creation of cover. This is obviously easiest to achieve for near-bank swims. On the Wensum syndicate water, the members draped willow branches over good near-bank runs where there was little natural foliage. Those branches quickly become permanent features, which formed

rafts in times of high water, and soon were reliable barbel-holding areas. The same ploy has worked for us on the Cherwell and the Bristol Avon. If you do create such a swim, it is a good idea, on the first few visits, not to fish it but simply to feed regularly. Fish will soon colonize the area and take up permanent residence.

In high water, both summer and winter, we have the premier conditions for barbel fishing. Coloured water can send them into a feeding frenzy and, if barbel are located, good catches can be accumulated. Again, it is the speed of flow that is important. What you should be looking for is smoothly flowing water of no more than walking pace. The depth is largely irrelevant. A barbel will feed confidently in eighteen inches of coloured water, whereas the same swim in clear conditions may be visited by the fish only after dark. High water leads to many interesting new swims being created. Creases become much more pronounced and are top-class areas at this time. Raft swims are formed round the bankside foliage and, provided that the current speed is suitable, these swims are also worth thorough investigation.

Slacker areas in the river, usually caused by mid-river obstructions, also come into their own more and more as the river rises, and this is when a bait placed in the smooth water behind rushes, boulders, or areas of collapsed bank can pay handsome dividends. Such obstructions create substantial boils a few yards below their positions, and this is extremely useful for locating snags that were previously unsuspected. The correct position for the bait will be a yard or two above the boil, which should see it directly behind the snag. Be prepared, however, to occasionally lose some gear when fishing swims of this nature.

The biggest mistake you can make when fishing in high water is to fish the dead slacks. As stated earlier, we do not rate still water for barbel fishing at any time. The fish do not need to move into the slacks simply because the current speed is increasing. While it is true that they will migrate to a more comfortable flow, the barbel are well adapted to holding their own in the heaviest currents. Even in a raging torrent, a depression in the gravel or the quieter water in the lee of a clump of streamer can be sufficient for the fish to hold its position quite easily.

As a general rule, as the current speed increases the barbel will shift their station to a flow of similar strength to that to which they are accustomed. Like chub, they move only as far as they need to achieve this objective. A good example of this behaviour is the famous Copse swim on the Wensum

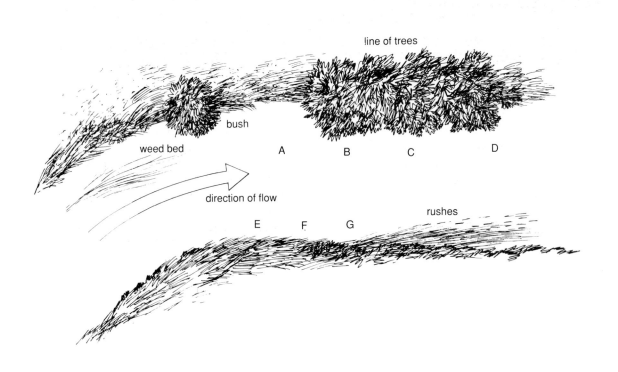

Copse swim on the Wensum.

A classic crease – the Boathouse on the Royalty.

(see the diagram). Under normal height and flow rates, the barbel are positioned at points A, B, C and D, under the trees. As the flow increases, a boil appears from the weedbed and bush at the head of the swim, as a direct result of increasing current speed and turbulence, and the barbel move across river to stations E, F and G. Very sluggish under normal conditions, this area now flows steadily and smoothly, giving the barbel a perfect operating base from which to forage for food. Understanding the effects of ever changing water conditions on the location and behaviour of barbel is a vital skill to acquire if you hope to enjoy any consistent success with the species.

3 Swim Preparation and Prebaiting

SUMMER TECHNIQUES

Without a shadow of doubt, the hours spent not actually fishing are the most vital in our barbel angling strategy. In the opening lines of the previous chapter we stated that most anglers are in far too great a hurry to start fishing. That was in the context of finding the swims to fish, admittedly, but the same comment has equal validity once the swims have been selected. We believe that if you wish to achieve any consistent success in barbel fishing the gravest mistake you can make is fishing swims prematurely, before any resident barbel have been given the chance to settle

A 9lb 12oz fish – the result of careful swim preparation.

into a confident feeding pattern. This is especially true in those areas where barbel have been observed. The less experienced barbel angler, having seen a group of fish over the gravel, cannot wait to begin fishing for them. With trembling fingers he baits his hook and then swings out the terminal rig to land just ahead of the fish. Heart thumping, he sits down to wait. As the minutes tick by, the excitement gradually wanes until, unable to resist the temptation any longer, our angler climbs to his feet again for another look into the water. He is amazed to see that the swim is barren, the barbel have departed. Obviously, those fish were not hungry, he thinks. The reality of the situation is that he wrecked his chances of catching those barbel right from the word go, by fishing for them. So what is our alternative?

The rule of thumb that we work to is so simple, and yet its importance cannot possibly be over emphasized. During the prebaiting process, the longer a swim is left undisturbed the greater are the chances of barbel colonizing the baited area. Having discovered the new food supply, the longer the fish are left to feed in peace the more confident they will become. Careful observation of feeding barbel has allowed us to identify other characteristics of their behaviour which have proved invaluable when the river has been too deep or murky to actually see the fish. When they first start to feed, they will invariably remain in the swim only for a short while before moving out for an excursion either up or down river. It is rather like the behaviour you see from a sparrow on the garden lawn, which takes a couple of beakfuls from a slice of bread and then flies off somewhere safe to eat it. It is an inbuilt instinct of wariness. However, the more visits the barbel make to the baited swim, without anything untoward occurring, such as an ounce bomb landing on their heads, the more they are

encouraged to remain longer in the vicinity. Gradually, their natural caution is overcome, until they are eventually resident there, at least while there is an adequate food supply. It is important to remember that word adequate. The two main reasons why the barbel may leave the swim are either that they have been alarmed or that there is no longer enough food to hold them there.

At that point, another aspect of their behaviour comes to the fore, of particular interest to the specialist barbel angler looking for the larger-than-average fish. The biggest fish present will often be the wariest, taking the longest to settle down into an enthusiastic feeding pattern. Logically, then, if you are after that elusive double, the longer the swim can be left unfished the greater will be your chances. Following on from that, the biggest fish present will, by definition, be one of the greediest. After all, it only became big by eating. Therefore, once it is feeding confidently, it will be the most avid feeder, often shouldering lesser individuals aside to get at the grub. We have used this trait to our advantage over recent seasons to take a tremendous number of large barbel. Our approach now is that if a very big fish is spotted in a swim we do not fish that swim at all in the daytime. Instead, it is periodically fed throughout the day in preparation for the introduction of a hookbait after dark. Our results to this tactic have been quite conclusive. On almost every occasion, the first bite has yielded the largest barbel present. Obviously, we are well aware that there may be circumstances where it is not possible to fish after dark, especially if the fishery rules do not permit it. In this case you have no alternative but to fish in daylight, but the rest of the advice remains sound, and we would rather content ourselves with two hours fishing towards dusk, with a high chance of success, than twelve hours of flogging away and spooking every barbel in the baited swims.

Let us now look at our prebaiting procedure in detail. There is no doubt at all that the premier attractant for barbel is hempseed, and any summer day will see at least a gallon used, to prime from six to eight swims. Initially, each of the selected areas will receive half a dozen bait droppers of hemp, whether or not barbel have actually been seen in the swim. We know that, if there are any barbel in the immediate vicinity, they will eventually move on to the hemp to feed, provided they are not disturbed. During this initial baiting we include samples of particles that make observation easy, and corn is the obvious choice, though pea-sized offerings of cheese or mini-boilies can be used with equal confidence.

When all the selected areas have been prebaited, it is time for quiet and patient observation of each one in turn. The visible particles give an indication of how fast the loose feed is being eaten, which is very important since the swims must be kept regularly topped up with bait if the barbel are to colonize them and become preoccupied and confident feeders. The frequency of topping up will also obviously depend on the level of activity in each individual area, not only by barbel but by all other species as well. Chub are particularly active over hemp, and they will devour a huge amount of the deposited bait. Although they can be a nuisance at times, taking baits meant for barbel, actively foraging chub will attract barbel into an area. When the time for fishing actually arrives, it is up to us to present our baits in such a way that they should be taken only by barbel. We can create the conditions for achieving this objective in the baiting procedure by establishing segregated feeding in the swim. Sweetcorn is particularly useful in this context. Chub will eat any amount of corn,

but barbel, on the other hand, on some rivers in certain circumstances, have been seen to be alarmed by large quantities. Although the barbel eat a number of corn grains they come across on those rivers, it is the hemp that is the premier attraction. This knowledge can be used to good effect. If a swim contains both feeding barbel and chub, it can be baited solely with hempseed plus an occasional grain of corn in one spot, and heavily baited with corn in another. On the Cherwell in the late 1980s, before the barbel became totally spooked by corn, this technique was used with such good effect that hardly any chub were landed, although the stretch contained hundreds of 12in corn crunchers. Most sessions saw totally segregated feeding. We repeat, however, that patience is the keyword. You must be prepared to spend hours of observation and regular feeding for this technique to be at its most effective. This separation of chub and barbel using sweetcorn does not work on all rivers, however, and it is a matter of trial and error to see what is the best technique for any particular fishery. On the Bristol Avon, for instance, the barbel eat corn by the bucketful.

A classic example of the above approach is the capture last season of a Great Ouse barbel of 12lb 6oz. This fish, with two other barbel, was observed under a far bank willow in mid-morning, and after the initial baiting there were also some thirty chub milling around, waiting to be fed again. By adopting the procedure outlined, the situation was achieved whereby the barbel were encouraged to feed under the far bank willow, and the chub led ten yards downstream. This took all the daylight hours, and no hookbait was introduced to the barbel until dusk. There was then only about thirty seconds to wait until the rod hammered over and the twelve-pounder was hooked. There was nothing particularly difficult about that capture, just the application of a lot of patience and a belief in a proven baiting technique. An impatient cast at midday, a hooked chub, and the chance at that monster barbel would most certainly have gone for that session.

During clear summer conditions, if you are going to present a hookbait in the daylight, then particle baits are the ones to use. Large traditional baits are taboo in clear water, and we have often seen barbel flee in terror from a piece of meat. For this reason, we never use large baits like luncheon meat in the daytime in clear water in prepared swims. There are two notable exceptions. The first is when fishing special paste or boilie baits after prebaiting, and the fish are preoccupied, at which time they lose their normal caution.

The second is the lobworm, which is a deadly barbel bait, and a freelined lob over a carpet of hemp can be equally effective, day or night. Large traditional baits, however, come into their own after dark, and a meat-based bait over the hemp carpet becomes a standard ploy. Even when no serious fishing is intended until after dark, we never prebait with such offerings. If a large chunk of luncheon meat is the intended offering, then the piece on the hook will be the first to be introduced. Again, lobs are an exception. Whether barbel actually eat the lobworms or not, they never appear to be spooked by them.

With particle baits there is a different approach. If the intended hookbait is the one you have used for observation – corn, for

A lovely Wensum double – 10lb 12oz.

instance – then there is no need for further elaboration. But if you intend to use tares, maple peas, or even a tiny scrap of meat, then free offerings are introduced in the bait dropper, along with the hempseed. The most obvious particles, of course, are maggots and casters, and these must be considered as a special case. As with hempseed, barbel will eat any quantity of them, and the more you put in the more likely you are to achieve a high concentration of fish. If maggots or casters are the intended hookbaits, then they will be used in similar quantities to the hemp. Again on the Cherwell, half a gallon of maggots and two pints of casters to each gallon of hemp was the approach used in the weeks following the capture of the twelve-pounder, with spectacular success. The barbel had become extremely spooky of corn, even in small amounts, and bunches of maggots over extensive hemp and maggot prebaiting became the order of the day. Although tremendously effective, heavy feeding with maggots and casters has two major drawbacks, in that it is both expensive and non-selective. All fish love maggots, and it is impossible to achieve segregated feeding when using them. You just have to be philosophical about the large number of indications from nuisance fish that are bound to result. You can reduce the problem substantially by using a large bunch on a big hook, and ignore all the little taps, but there is not much you can do about the odd kamikaze chub.

It will do no harm to state again that, if at all possible, the most effective way to fish for barbel in the summer months is to spend the daylight hours preparing the ground, not even attempting to fish until the light intensity begins to fade. After dark, the serious fishing begins. To the casual observer it would seem that we adopt an extremely lazy approach to our barbel fishing. Rarely are we out of bed until perhaps mid-morning, and then it is time for a very large, casual and relaxed breakfast. After the meal, a slow wander along the river bank, putting bait here and there, and generally taking life easily, is followed by a trip back to the van for a midday cup of tea. In the afternoon, we may have a go for any average-size barbel that have been located, to try out new rigs and tactics perhaps, in between several other baiting and observation sessions. Tea time brings another trip back to the van for a large evening meal, to sustain us for the long night to come. At about half an hour before dark, each swim receives a heavy final baiting. As darkness approaches, most of the casual observers will have retired homewards, and that is when our whole attitude changes. Now our barbel fishing takes on a new intensity, a new meaning, and many hours of hard work, fishing to a predetermined pattern, lie ahead of us. You will have to read the next chapter to find out what this pattern is.

WINTER TECHNIQUES

The increased flow and depth and the decreasing clarity of the winter river mean that more water is capable of holding feeding barbel. A stretch of river with perhaps only two swims where barbel are found consistently in the summer may now feature a dozen or more glides, all of ideal characteristics. Such areas may only be eighteen inches of gin-clear open water in summer, over smooth gravel, perhaps visited by barbel only after dark, but in the winter, with some colour and a foot or more extra depth of steadily moving flow, they become ideal holding spots, where barbel may feed happily all day. The prebaiting technique we employ in the winter therefore reflects the greater number of location possibilities.

It is true to say that, in normal summer conditions, the essential features of a reliable swim will usually include reasonable depth and good cover near at hand. A hookbait will need to be placed accurately in order to achieve consistent catches. Even after dark in the summer, when they are certainly most active, barbel largely remain in the same few swims unless disturbed. The good winter swim, however, is largely controlled by one factor alone, and that is the speed of flow. A comfortable steady glide of constantly smooth surface is the ideal, and the best summer swim will be vacated if the extra push of water makes it too fast and turbulent.

In the winter, therefore, with many more places on the river where the barbel could be located, our prebaiting is more concerned with preparing sections of river as opposed to defined and fairly restricted swims. As a general rule, we would probably deposit loose feed in three or four times as many different spots in the winter, but use a lot less feed initially in each one. We are trying to achieve the effect of having feed available to any barbel on the stretch in the hope of encouraging them to forage for more.

The catches on the Bristol Avon last winter provide a good illustration of the technique in practice. The previous summer, a willow had toppled into the river, creating a superb summer swim, with all the cover the fish could require. Over twenty barbel, many of them large, took up

Another absolute cracker from the Bristol Avon weighing in at 10lb 14oz.

residence under that feature, and we were able to entice individual fish from under the cover by careful feeding and precise positioning of the hookbait. The winter saw an interesting transformation. The increased push of water, coupled with the increase in depth, meant that the broken flow through the willow branches created extreme turbulence in the summer holding spot, resulting in the barbel vacating the area completely. However, some forty yards below the tree there commenced a long steady glide, less than a foot deep in the summer, but now ideal home for the shoal. We were to discover that the shoal had split into two groups, at different stations along the glide, and by feeding the top and bottom of the swim we were able to take barbel from each position. The technique was to feed both areas and then make one cast only into one of them. After a fish had been taken, that spot was then fed again and rested while the other was fished, and so on. In that way, several catches of over a dozen fish were taken.

Let us now look at our winter feeding technique in detail. The first point to make is that if a good summer swim appears to meet all the criteria of a good winter one then it can be baited exactly as it was in the summer. There is no doubt that it will still contain barbel, if the flow rate is acceptable. It is in the long smooth runs and glides, many of them apparently featureless, that a different approach is called for. Say there is a hundred-yard smooth run, over clean gravel and about four feet in depth. We know that swim will contain barbel somewhere along its length, but we do not know exactly where. What we do is walk the length and deposit two bait droppers of hemp every ten yards or so. Areas will be baited both near and far bank, as well as in mid-river, and by this means we know that any barbel in that particular section of river will find it impossible to move

more than a few yards before coming across one of our piles of bait. During this blanket baiting of the run, any obvious spot, for instance where the current is slowed by mid-river rushes, may receive more bait, on the assumption that this may be the holding spot for the barbel in the area. When a stretch of river is a succession of obvious features, connected by smooth glides, then not only are the main swims baited but the runs in between as well. In good conditions in winter, barbel are more inclined to move around in daylight than they were in summer, and odd individuals will be caught as they move between the main swims. It will stand repeating that the whole point of the technique is having bait available at any point we feel may lie on a barbel's patrol route.

The good conditions we refer to would comprise a coloured river, with a water temperature on an upward gradient and in excess of 44°F (7°C). Under these circumstances, barbel are actively searching for food, and in actual fact they meet us half way in the location process. By prebaiting every few yards, and then fishing in a very mobile manner, which we shall be covering later, we know that a barbel and our hookbait must be on a collision course. It is simply a matter of time, provided that you have no objection of working hard at your fishing. That is the absolute crux of the matter. Our systematic prebaiting approach is hard work, involving a lot of walking, and you must have an absolute belief in the principles behind it and be prepared to persevere. Each area must be visited and rebaited several times in a day for the method to be at its most effective, as it is absolutely vital to be as sure as it is possible to be that all the prebaited areas contain some feed at all times. The actual fishing technique, to be discussed later, depends entirely on this belief.

The diagram illustrates a typical swim to

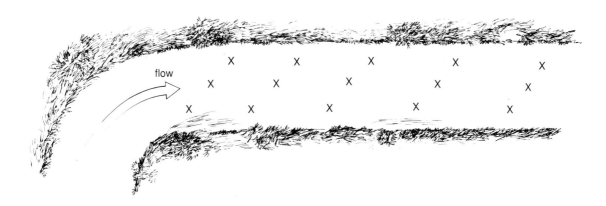

A suitable swim for systematic baiting.

which the foregoing technique would be applicable. What it shows is a smoothly flowing hundred-yard long straight, coming off a shallow bend. All the positions marked with an X would receive an initial feed of two dropper-loads of hemp apiece, and would each be rebaited at regular intervals during the session. Once one particular spot produces a barbel bite, or a barbel rolls, it is a reasonable assumption that other fish may be present, and the baiting will then be increased in that swim.

Can we again stress that the foregoing prebaiting technique is one that is recommended for winter conditions that are reasonable to good. As the winter river becomes lower, clearer, and possibly colder, catching barbel becomes progressively more hit and miss, as they become torpid and will not move onto bait, and the value of prebaiting large sections of river considerably more uncertain. In clear water there is no method to beat the swimfeeder for effectiveness, at least in the daylight, and if the temperature is still reasonable, say over about 40°F (4°C), there is nothing wrong in placing dropper-loads of maggots in several interesting-looking areas. Having said that, maggot fishing for barbel is at its best

when there is a high concentration of bait in one area, continuously being topped up. Our feeder approach is invariably one of selecting a good glide and then building up the swim by very regular recasting. If the water temperature suggests that the barbel should be fairly active, the swim can also be given additional injections of maggots occasionally, via the bait dropper, at the head of the run. For this fishing, half a gallon of maggots per day would be the absolute minimum, and we frequently use as much as a gallon. Again, hard work reaps its own rewards.

Feeder fishing during the day in clear water is an excellent way of prebaiting in readiness for the dark hours, where night fishing is allowed. As with clear summer conditions in daytime, large baits are very ineffective, and may even spook the fish, but after dark it is a very different story. More often than we can count we have fished swims after dark which have been continuously fed with maggots all day, and taken several barbel on meat baits or lobs. That raises another important point. If you do intend to fish at night, it is worth employing the same prebaiting technique as described for coloured water, with hemp,

Getting down to it on the Severn!

Autumn eleven-pounder from the Cherwell.

but not even commencing to fish until the dark hours. Many are the mild winter days, when the water has been too clear for good daytime fishing with large baits, when we have fished exactly as we do in the summer, baiting up in the day and then fishing in earnest from dusk onwards. With adequate water temperature, and provided that you are dressed warmly, with waterproof outer garments, night fishing for barbel in the winter is perhaps the most productive of all.

It is when the river is low and clear, and the temperature below 40°F (4°C) that barbel fishing is at its grimmest, and these days we do not bother trying. Other species are much more worthwhile quarries under these circumstances. However, if you insist on fishing for barbel, our advice would be not to prebait at all. The barbel will not be encouraged to search for food anyway, no matter what you do, so any loose feed would simply be wasted. The only worthwhile alternative is to fish a known barbel swim with the feeder, using a very small quantity of maggots.

Better still, go pike fishing!

4 Summer Fishing Techniques

FISHING IN DAYLIGHT

In the previous chapter, we emphasized the fact that the most effective approach to summer fishing is to bait all day and fish after dark. If carried out correctly, that method virtually guarantees success. We recognize, however, that not everybody will be able, or indeed willing, to fish at night, and so let us look first of all at the techniques that can be employed to tempt a barbel or two from the low clear water of a summer's day.

With the notable exception of that most universally accepted natural bait, lobworm, daytime fishing in the summer is best carried out with particle baits, unless heavy rain has put colour in the water. In

A six-pounder taken from the Kennet on a summer's night.

those circumstances, large meaty baits are just as effective in summer as they are in the winter.

Assuming that you have followed our advice on prebaiting, and the barbel in a swim have been given at least a reasonable period to feed undisturbed on your chosen particles, the fish will be receptive to the hookbaits. However, this will only be the case if the terminal rig does not alarm the fish, and if the presentation of the bait itself does not arouse the barbel's suspicions.

In low clear water, these points are obviously the entire key to success or failure.

The Problem of Line Bites

Apart from keeping yourself as unobtrusive as possible, the most potentially alarming item is going to be the line itself, where it rises from the terminal tackle to the rod point. If the prebaiting job has been done efficiently, and there are a group of avidly feeding barbel in attendance, especially in shallow water, it is impossible to totally eliminate line bites, caused when the fish brush against the line as they mill around over the feed. It is important, though, to ensure that this problem is minimized, since it takes very little time for all the fish to become badly spooked.

Trefor has a recurrent nightmare about a never-to-be-forgotten evening on the Wensum. Three huge barbel came on to the bait just before dark, and about half an hour later a hookbait was lowered into the swim. Unluckily, the lead touched a barbel on its descent. Mere seconds later, three great looping line bites were experienced as the three big fish left the swim via the exit channel in the weedbed. Talk about being frustrated! That was an important lesson learned on how easily the fish can be alarmed by line, which will be made much worse by striking at line indications that are not true bites.

Liners must be differentiated from the real thing, and the only way, apart from actually seeing a fish foul the line with either its body or fins, is to hold the line at all times. A real bite will draw the line, usually after an initial pluck or relaxation of tension, whereas a liner nods the rod top with no preliminary indication and on most occasions with no obvious pull being felt at the reel.

There are so many subtle differences in line bite indications, however, that the above can be no more than a simplified guide to a difficult problem. We would emphasize that no strike should be attempted if you are not sure whether an indication is a liner or not. If it was a real bite and the fish left undisturbed, it will continue feeding and give you another opportunity. If, however, the indication was false, and struck at, you may have wrecked your chance of catching that particular barbel and almost certainly alarmed the remaining group of fish. Sorting out the problem of line bites is the one aspect that is very difficult to describe on paper. In this regard there is no substitute for practical experience. Particularly important is being able to watch barbel in clear water. If you can actually see the reaction of fish to touching the line and note the indications given on rod top and fingers, it will help you differentiate between all the various differing indications you could experience when you cannot see the fish.

The more line you have on the bottom between rod and bait, and the narrower the line angle, the less will be the incidence of line bites. For these reasons, it is advisable to have the rod point as close to the surface of the water as possible, a few yards upstream of where the fish are feeding. A swanshot a few feet above the terminal lead and hooklink helps to ensure that the line is hard on the riverbed.

Soft Hooklink Materials

Anyone who has watched barbel feeding at close quarters can be in no doubt that their sensitive barbules easily detect the presence of stiff monofilament line adjacent to the bait. Hookbaits may be ignored for this reason alone, but it is obviously dangerous to revert to light line for these most powerful of adversaries, especially in snaggy situations. The answer partly lies with modern, soft hooklink materials and, in our opinion, the best available at the moment are Drennan Dacron and Sufix Herculine, the latter being amazingly thin, strong and supple. A hook length of 12–18in would normally be used.

Buoyant Baits and Counterbalanced Hooks

When barbel have not been fished for very often, they are receptive initially to baits fished static on the bottom, hoovering them up quite confidently along with the loose feed. It takes very few fish to be caught, however, for them to start to wise up, and bait presentation becomes a critical factor. The same fish that were browsing quite sedately over the gravel will now constantly flash and fan their large fins, creating turbulence and underwater vortices. This disturbance lifts all the loose offerings off the bottom, and anything that does not behave as it should, such as a hookbait attached to line and a heavy hook, is shunned. We have both been driven to distraction countless times on the Wensum by this behaviour, which has usually resulted in all the feed being taken in a swim apart from that on the hook. This, obviously, is a highly unsatisfactory state of affairs. The problem is, then, how to make our hookbaits behave as naturally as the free offerings.

The first thing we can try is the hair rig,

using a very fine hair of about half an inch. This arrangement certainly gives the chosen bait a limited amount of free travel, allowing it to behave more naturally, but after extensive trial we have formed the opinion that this approach has more drawbacks than it does advantages for the bulk of our barbel fishing. For a start, unlike in carp fishing with large boilies, particle baits are largely non-selective. If they are mounted on a big hook, then all the taps and knocks from such things as gudgeon and small dace can be ignored, while you wait for the barbel to come along. The hair rig is different. These small fish can get the whole bait in their mouths easily, resulting in multitudes of false bites and stolen baits. Even when the swim contains barbel only, we have not found the hair to be the benefit that we expected. The problem has not been one of not getting bites, but of missing them when they do occur. Study of the barbel's feeding pattern gave us the clue to what was happening. Even when it is feeding confidently, an individual fish will remain on the feed only for short periods before drifting out of the swim to swallow what he has just picked up. Within a short while, he will be back, and this process will continue all day if the barbel are left undisturbed. It seems very likely that when a fish moves out of the swim it does so with the bait held in its lips only. Obviously, as the line tightens suddenly and the quivertip pulls round you have to strike. As often as not, though, the hook is not in the mouth at all, and the strike results in a missed and badly spooked barbel, a possibly broken hair, and the end to your chances in that swim for a while. So the hair has not been the answer for us.

Having established that it is preferable to fish for barbel with baits mounted directly on the hook in the conventional manner, we have to consider how else we can effect

Summer barbel on the gravel shallows.

a natural presentation. There are two answers to this dilemma – the use of naturally buoyant baits and the use of baits fished on buoyant hooks. As far as buoyant baits are concerned, the presentation is one that works along the same principle as pop-up boilies in carp fishing. The bait can be made either permanently buoyant, in which case it will always fish at a fixed distance above the bottom, controlled by an appropriately positioned split shot, or of neutral buoyancy, such that the weight of the hook is only just sufficient to hold the bait on the bottom, but turbulence will lift it as naturally as the free particles. Any of

the normal baits can be made either buoyant or neutral by the addition of small pieces of polystyrene on the hook. Neutral buoyancy baits are the most fiddly to get just right, but it is well worth the trouble as they can be deadly, and have solved presentation problems on many of our barbel rivers.

If you are going to fish neutral buoyancy, however, it is far better to prepare accurately counterbalanced hooks at home, rather than becoming more and more exasperated on the bank, attempting to trim tiny chunks of polystyrene to exactly the correct size for every rebaiting. Making a hook of neutral buoyance is simplicity it-self. Attach a thin sliver of cork to the back of the hook shank, initially by the tiniest amount of glue possible. Enough cork should be used at first to float the hook when placed in a clear glass of water. Then trim off small pieces of cork with a sharp blade – a Stanley knife is ideal – and check the flotation after each trimming. When the hook just, and only just, starts to sink, it is as close to water density as possible. At that point the hook is dried and made more secure by a thin sliver of glue along the base of the cork. All that remains is to ap-ply a layer of clear varnish to the cork, to prevent it from becoming waterlogged in use, and you have a hook perfectly bal-anced, whatever size bait you decide to

use. The underlying principle is so simple. As the hook is to all intents and purposes weightless, any hookbait will react to underwater disturbance exactly as do simi-lar unfettered bait items. The barbel will have little reason to be suspicious of it, tak-ing the bait quite confidently as it rises in the water with the other particles.

A fond memory is two barbel on the Cherwell, which were feeding quite frenziedly on hemp and corn one hot August afternoon. For quite some time, three grains of corn on an ordinary size 6 Au Lion d'Or had been stubbornly re-fused, every other grain in the vicinity hav-ing been devoured with great gusto. Those two barbel had seen it all before, constantly flashing over the gravel, making puffs of silt

Matt Hayes loose feeds an Ouse barbel swim.

rise, lifting the hemp and corn off the bottom – all except for the hookbait, of course. Eventually, it was decided to try a weightless hook, and the next time the barbel temporarily left the swim three corn grains were introduced, this time on a size 6 that had been doctored with cork as explained above. The difference this made was remarkable. Within minutes, the barbel were back. The bait behaved exactly as planned. As soon as turbulence was created, the bait lifted very invitingly and the smaller barbel took it without hesitation. Seven pounds thirteen ounces that fish weighed, a very satisfying capture indeed. Half an hour later, the second barbel was similarly fooled, but this time the end result was not quite so happy. This fish, which looked close to double figures, made for some tree roots, and that was that. The efficiency of weightless hooks, however, had been established beyond doubt. Outwitting those fish was all about understanding an angling problem and then solving it.

Even with the very delicate presentations possible with the modifications just outlined, however, it does not take long for barbel to sort them out as well, and then even buoyant baits will be ignored. Worse still, the barbel may actually flee in terror from a particular bait if they have had a bad experience with it. This was mentioned earlier in the context of using large baits such as luncheon meat in clear water, but the same behaviour has been observed with particle baits after they have been used for a while. This is particularly true of sweetcorn. On both the Wensum and the Cherwell, where the barbel population has experienced the full range of our expertise, we have watched a shoal of barbel scatter in fright at coming across only a few grains of corn in a swim. Remember, though, that we are talking about fish that have been pursued intently for a long time. When this situation has

been reached it is time for another rethink to keep us one step ahead of the barbel.

Hempseed Hookbaits

Despite what was said earlier about the hair rig, this is the one time when it has a useful application. Barbel never spook at hemp, no matter how often they have been fished for. They simply cannot leave it alone, and a bait consisting entirely of hempseed will often succeed when other particles have failed. Hemp can be fished in its seed form in three ways, as shown in the diagram. The simplest way is to superglue a cluster of seeds on the hook itself, or form a cluster round a short hair, as shown. Both of these alternatives obviously result in a larger bait than ocurrs naturally. Perhaps the best way of presenting hemp as a hookbait, when the quarry are nervous barbel, is to superglue individual seeds on a multi-hair arrangement, as illustrated. Several good Wensum fish have fallen for this

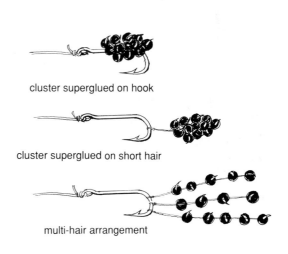

cluster superglued on hook

cluster superglued on short hair

multi-hair arrangement

Hook rigs for using hemp.

Trefor fishes the Bristol Avon.

ruse. The obvious drawback is that it is extremely fiddly. When we intend to fish in this manner we prepare in advance enough hairs for several rebaitings.

Fishing large Baits over Hemp

Another successful ploy, when barbel have become frightened of certain particles, is almost the exact opposite of the hempseed fishing. It is to fish a large single natural bait over the hemp carpet. The bait *par excellence* is undoubtedly lobworms, which barbel love. The first double-figure Cherwell barbel that we ever caught showed the value of the humble lob. A group of fish had been pursued for several weeks, with singular lack of success. In the exceptionally low and clear water, every trick in the book had been tried with particle baits, but the barbel would have none of them. Corn, casters, tares, maggots and miniboilies had all been tried, on all the rig variations mentioned, but to no avail. When lobs were eventually used one early September afternoon, after some very welcome rain had allowed our stocks to be replenished, the reaction was completely different. Four fish in quick succession picked up the worms very confidently, the best going 10lb 3oz. Obviously, the barbel had no reason to suspect the lobs as dangerous. Many fish have since fallen to this technique, and a recommended refinement is to inject a little air into the tail of the worm, which makes it waver in the current, just off the riverbed, very invitingly. Sometimes it is just too inviting. The first time we tried this ploy on the Cherwell, a jet-propelled three-quarter-pound trout came out of nowhere and rocketed off with the bait in what can only be described as a confident manner.

Heavy Baiting with Maggots and Casters

There is a third approach to barbel that have become wary and difficult to tempt on particles, but it is expensive. The method, however, is applicable only on those rivers that do no have a significant eel problem.

Where maggots and casters are used in small amounts, the same problems exist as with using things such as corn and tares. However, if they are introduced in much larger quantities – say, up to about a gallon in a single swim – the barbel become totally preoccupied with them and can become ridiculously easy to catch. Once they are turned on to maggots, much of the barbel's caution deserts them, and the result is often fish after fish, despite the disturbance created by landing fish and regular introductions of feed.

Again, the Cherwell provides a perfect illustration of this in practice. In 1989, the week after Tony's twelve-pounder was taken, the barbel were spooking badly

The Cherwell twelve-pounder is returned to fight another day.

at the sight of corn. On this occasion the use of both hempseed hookbaits and lobs proved unproductive, and on the second day it was decided to try heavy baiting with maggots and casters. The technique was to prebait with hemp as usual, but, over the first few hours, to add about six pints of maggots and two of casters. Just before the introduction of a hookbait, another two pints of mixed maggots and casters was lowered into the swim, to be followed by a feeder rig, with a large bunch of about fifteen maggots on a size 6 hook.

The very first bite to this new approach turned out to be the second biggest we have taken from the river, a cracking 11¼-pounder. In the weeks that followed that exciting capture the technique was refined even more, with even larger amounts of maggots being used, and a very large number of barbel were taken, including catches of five and six fish from a single swim in a very short space of time. Several recaptures, a phenomenon that underlines the importance of being able to recognize individual fish and which will be discussed in depth later, demonstrated how preoccupied the fish had become, and these were barbel that only a few weeks earlier were almost impossible to tempt.

At this point it will do no harm to recap on the last few paragraphs, and put them in their proper context. You need to resort to these more specialized techniques only where educated barbel become unreceptive to a more orthodox approach. Let us draw a parallel here with modern carp fishing. There is little point in embarking on an expensive boilie campaign in a lightly fished pool, where the carp would happily accept lobs or freelined flake. Similarly, do not fall into the trap, not to mention the cost, of thinking that you must be armed with gallons of maggots when your particular barbel will be quite happy to pick up corn from the riverbed. Use the simple

approach first. Only when that fails need you start to introduce more refinements.

The Importance of Multiple Swim Preparation

One particularly fascinating aspect of barbel behaviour was discovered, almost by accident, during our fishing on the Wensum. Careful observation led us to the conclusion that barbel became wary of certain baits only in those swims in which they had had a nasty experience. Individual barbel which spooked at corn in one swim which had been extensively fished would quite happily pick up exactly the same bait in another area they considered safe. This was not observed just once but many times, and it has been used to our advantage since. In fact, much of our fishing has been shaped by this knowledge. For a long time we were of the opinion that once a barbel had departed a swim in haste, because it had been startled by something, it would refuse to feed for a long time before returning to the swim again. This assumption we now know to be wrong. By baiting several swims in fairly close proximity to one another, on the Wensum initially and subsequently on both the Cherwell and the Bristol Avon, we now know that a barbel that has been spooked out of a swim will begin feeding in the next available baited area it comes across. It may well take some time to return to the swim in which it received its fright, but in the meantime will feed in the second area quite happily. This is not conjecture; we have seen it happen many times. Deliberate fish scaring on the Wensum gave us sufficient proof that we had uncovered something of great significance. An easily recognized barbel was purposely startled so that it shot out of the swim downstream. The next available pile of bait was about ten yards away, and a hookbait was waiting among the loose feed. Within a minute, the rod top bent round and eventually the same barbel that had just vacated the first area was being swung ashore. Fascinating, isn't it?

This knowledge obviously extends the useful life of any approach to the fishing. That barbel associate certain swims with danger only with certain baits is perhaps difficult to understand but it is a fact. This is obviously another very strong reason why you should have several swims primed simultaneously, if angling pressure permits. It is all about having an edge, keeping one step ahead of the fish.

Selective Fishing for the Biggest Barbel

So far in this treatise about summer fishing in the daytime we have talked about the problems of getting a bite from a barbel, any barbel. Let us now look a little deeper into how we can fish selectively for the biggest barbel in any particular swim. We have already outlined methods of creating segregated feeding during the prebaiting process, with particular reference to keeping chub away from our barbel baits. What we are now trying to achieve during the actual fishing is preventing the smaller barbel from taking the bait. There are two ways of doing this, one relying on loose-feed positioning, the other on hookbait manipulation.

For the first, let us assume that we have a group of barbel actively feeding over the hemp. If we observe their comings and goings for a while, it is very noticeable that the biggest fish present is often the first to return to the swim, once all the fish are feeding confidently. We also see that the fish always enter the swim at the same point. What we can now do, as well as keeping the main body of feed topped up, is to drop perhaps one bait dropper of hemp at the position in the swim at which

the barbel enter it. If a hookbait is very accurately placed at the same point, it is now almost certain that the first barbel with an opportunity to take that bait will be the big one. You could, of course, be lucky enough to take the biggest fish by simply fishing a hookbait over the main body of the hemp but, as this feed will probably be much more scattered, that will be very hit-and-miss and much less certain of success. There will be no way of knowing at exactly which point over the hemp the biggest fish will choose to feed. Obviously, in any group of fish the biggest may exhibit a different pattern of behaviour from the one described. The whole point is that patient observation over a long time will enable you to work out where to put a hookbait so that the fish you are after will be the most likely to take it, narrowing the odds in your favour.

It is also vitally important to know when to introduce the hookbait. After working out, after hours of carefully study of the barbel's behaviour, where a bait should be placed to tempt that massive fish you can see, there is little point in dropping a lump of lead on its head. That will wreck everything you have been working for. The hookbait must be introduced to the appropriate position when the barbel is not there. Your hours of observation will have confirmed their habit of continually commuting to and from the swim, and the time to get the bait into position is when they have temporarily vacated the area. If possible, the bait should be lowered rather than dropped, hence our earlier advice about preparing near-bank swims. On the Wensum, the plop of a single swanshot being dropped in was enough to spook the barbel and make them abandon the swim for a long time. A hurried or clumsy move will undo the work of many patient hours. On that point, it is a good idea to practise on a group of average-sized barbel, as we have

An Upper Severn seven.

done over the last five seasons. By establishing what they will or will not stand for, you will have the best chance of making the right move at the right time when the chance of that elusive double comes along. It is a simple matter of eliminating all possible mistakes. If you do nothing wrong, then success is guaranteed.

Perhaps the most exciting way to fish selectively for a big barbel is to manoeuvre the hookbait manually in such a way that only the fish you are after is allowed to have it. To achieve this, the two essentials are clear water, in which the fish are easily observed, and an easily visible hookbait. Again, corn is an obvious choice. With the hookbait in position, sit as quietly and inconspicuously as possible, while able to see everything that is happening in the

swim. Get yourself comfortable, with a little slack line held in the fingers of your left hand. Eventually, a barbel will approach the bait. If he appears about to take it and is not the fish you are after, give the bait a little tweak by pulling the line. Such a small adjustment will not usually throw a bad scare into the fish, but will be enough to prevent the bait actually being taken. This process can continue indefinitely until the desired barbel is seen to take the bait. Your reaction to that is obvious, though there is no need to wait for an actual bite. If a barbel has been seen to take the bait, strike at once.

One word of warning on this approach. Barbel are easily deterred from taking a bait by these small movements of the line. However, chub are a very different kettle of fish. Inducing a take from chub by bait movement is a well documented and deadly technique. Far from discouraging a chub from taking your barbel bait, a tweak on the line could actually encourage a very savage take – exactly what you don't want. Take our advice. If you fancy this kind of exciting barbel fishing, it is well worth going to the trouble of creating segregated feeding, as described earlier, before positioning your barbel bait. If, however, despite all your efforts, there are chub feeding alongside the barbel, the best thing to do if a chub picks up the hookbait is nothing. As often as not, the chub will feel the line and drop the bait, leaving it intact. Our record is two grains of corn being picked up and dropped by chub no less than eight times before they were eventually accepted by a barbel of 8lb 14oz. There is little you can do if a chub insists on galloping off with the bait, except to hope that it's a five-pounder. This selective fishing for the biggest barbel in a group is heart-thumping cat-and-mouse stuff, requiring tremendous restraint and self-control, but there is little in angling that is more exciting.

Playing Barbel

Many of the fish of the summer months are going to be hooked in close proximity to weedbeds or other forms of cover, giving easy opportunities for the barbel to snag the line. Earlier in this book we discussed the strength of tackle needed to give ourselves the best chance of landing these, the most powerful of our river coarse fish.

A Bristol Avon barbel battles for its freedom.

49

However, the strongest gear in the world will prove useless if you allow the fish to go where it likes and dictate the proceedings. If you have adequate power at your command, make sure that you use it to the full.

What all this is leading up to is a discussion on the rival merits of backwinding and playing fish from the clutch. The only application we can see for backwinding, which is essentially overriding the clutch mechanism, is where a hooklink is being employed which is of substantially lower breaking strain than the main line. For instance, much of our stillwater roach fishing is carried out using a spool of 6lb main line, both for convenience and shock resistance when casting heavy feeders, in conjunction with 2lb hooklinks. In these circumstances, using the clutch can be dangerous. Even if it is set to slip before the breaking strain of the lighter link is reached, the inertia at the reel is often such that a sudden plunge from the fish at close range may see that breaking strain temporarily exceeded before the clutch yields, leading to a crack-off. Only with very light links to heavier main line is this a problem.

Obviously, with barbel fishing, the above is not relevant. The much heavier lines required ensure that the inertia factor is insignificant, and we believe that it is crazy not to use a modern fixed-spool reel in the manner for which it was designed when fishing for barbel. There is no doubt at all in our minds that the angler does not exist, no matter how experienced, who will allow the tackle to exert its maximum pressure on a fish before giving line manually. We cannot see the point in any angler equipping himself with a powerful carbon rod, perhaps costing in the region of £100, and a superbly engineered fixed-spool, such as an ABU, Shimano or Mitchell, and then refusing to use the power of the rod and screwing tight the clutch mechanism and overriding it. If you are going to shovel line up the rod rings the moment the rod bends more than a few degrees you might as well save yourself a lot of money and use a garden cane and a cotton reel.

Seriously, we cannot stress too strongly that you will be well advised to learn how to use the clutch properly, to be able, with confidence, to allow your tackle to do the job it was designed for. Forget the prophets of doom who tell you that a clutch imparts line twist. In thirty years of intense big-fish angling, this has never been a problem for us. Even if it were, if you change your line as often as you should the problem is irrelevant anyway.

The clutch should be set so that a barbel has to battle for every yard of line that it wins, and the rod will normally be bent to about a quarter-circle before the clutch begins to yield. If there is appreciably less or more deflection than that for a particular strength of line, then the tackle is unbalanced and you are using too stiff or too sloppy a rod respectively.

Another weakness with backwinding, even if you are capable of allowing the rod to utilize its power, is during a fast, irresistible run, when you have to yield line to avoid being broken. A wildly backwardly spinning reel handle means that you have lost all control, and it is very difficult to regain this control without actually grabbing the handle and bringing the fish up with a jerk, which will often result in a smash or a hook pulling out. With a properly set clutch, a fast powerful run can be controlled by steadily increased finger pressure on the spool. This steady pressure build-up means that you are in command of the situation, and not the barbel, and is much less likely to result in disaster. Obviously, in a situation where you have to stop a fish or have it deeply in a snag, finger pressure on the spool can be increased to maximum, preventing any line from being taken.

The first Cherwell double, weighing 10lb 3oz.

We realize that, after reading this, you will still play the barbel in the way you want and with which you feel most comfortable. But heed this warning. If you play barbel in snaggy situations by backwinding, there will come a day, possibly with that fish of a lifetime, when you will bitterly regret it.

51

Quivertips

Although we use a range of quivertips for the bulk of our barbel fishing, fitted with Betalights as shown in the diagram, and some of the winter techniques in particular would be much more ineffective without them, summer fishing during the day with particles is the one circumstance in which they are often dispensed with. The reason is this. With these smaller baits, taps and plucks from small nuisance fish are a fact of life you just have to put up with. With a quivertip, even a 3oz version, some of the pulls from dace, gudgeon, small roach and so on can be surprisingly strong, putting a respectable bend into the tip. Unless you have nerves of steel, you can be tempted into an unwarranted strike, resulting in nothing more than spooking the barbel you have been patiently weaning onto the bait, perhaps for several hours. For this reason, in swims where the barbel cannot be

Betalight adaptor for fitting direct to rod top

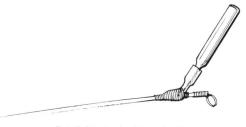

Betalight attached to quivertip

Use of Betalights.

watched actually picking up the bait, we will often fish directly off the rod top. The attentions of small fish are then much more distinguishable, as rattly plucks only. Sit back and relax. Despite what you may have read, confidently feeding barbel will give you a good solid thump, which is totally unmistakable. Every single one of the large number of barbel that we have taken from several rivers this season left us in no doubt whatever that it wanted the bait.

Retaining Barbel

In Chapter 1 we stated that there is nothing wrong in retaining barbel in good carp sacks while setting up the equipment for a photograph. In fact, we said that their use was recommended to make sure that the barbel recovers fully from the vigours of the fight before being returned to a possibly strongly flowing river. In very warm summer weather, however, please be extra careful that you use these receptacles with common sense. If you place a large barbel in a sack in only inches of shallow, stagnant water, which is possibly very de-oxygenated and exposed to the hot sun, the fish is going to suffer undue stress. You must find water of decent depth and with a steady flow. Only if the fish is able to pass ample oxygen through its gills while resting in the sack is it going to recover fully. Go to the trouble of staking the sack in such a way that the barbel is facing upstream, and has room to move without the sack clinging too tightly round it. As with all things in angling, please act responsibly.

FISHING AT NIGHT

The light is now fading fast. All day, we have been walking the banks, feeding barbel in several swims, sitting around taking

An immaculate, scale-perfect Kennet fish.

our ease, just watching. There has been time for plenty of rest, a leisurely meal, and even a little sunbathing. Our tackle is all checked and prepared; nothing has been left to chance. Now the time for idleness is past. In the gathering gloom, like vampires, we are coming alive. A new urgency overwhelms us. It is time to search for our first victim.

In Chapter 3 we mentioned a definite fishing pattern for the dark hours, so let us now examine that pattern in detail. The first thing to understand is that if the swims have remained unfished all day a bite can be expected immediately a bait is introduced, provided that the bait is carefully lowered into position and not cast in clumsily. This emphasizes the importance of preparing swims at exactly one rod length from the bank. In the darkness it is a simple matter to place the bait in exactly the correct position by extending the rod over the water and simply lowering the bait into the swim. No guesswork is involved; the terminal tackle will land on the carpet of hemp every time.

Unless eels are a problem, the bait will invariably be meat-based or lobworm. Unlike in daylight, such baits will not alarm the fish at night, as they obviously feed less by sight and more by smell; nor will they be alarmed by the bait entering the swim while they are in residence unless undue disturbance is created. If eels are very active, they can become a real nuisance, but the comfort we draw from eel activity is that, on those nights when they are active, the barbel are too. Using much larger baits than normal is one way of minimizing the eel problem. Although they will still peck at the baits, they are often unable to take them properly, giving the barbel at least a fighting chance of finding them. Perhaps more important, if an eel bite is strong enough for us to be forced into a strike, the large bait usually results in the fish being missed, which is liable to prove a lot less disturbing to any barbel present than a hooked eel thrashing about in the water. Generally speaking, though, when eels are really on the prowl, it is probably more sensible to stick to baits that are less attractive to them, such as corn, tares, or any of the hemp-based pastes mentioned in Chapter 1. With particle baits after dark, we give each swim a little longer before moving on, as the barbel often do not home in on particles quite so quickly as they do to more obvious meat-based offerings.

It is probably relevant at this point to say a few brief words about other ways of minimizing the problem of eels, as they can drive you to distraction at times. Each swim will hold only so many of these tackle-tangling horrors, and we have often embarked on an eel removal exercise in the last two hours of daylight, by fishing for them deliberately with lobs. It does cut down the problem after dark considerably, but of course you have to weigh up whether the disturbance caused to the swim is compensated for by more eel-free fishing in the dark hours. It is a difficult equation to solve, and you can never be sure you are doing the right thing. Perhaps better, and certainly much simpler, less disturbing, and considerably less effort, is to peg out deadbaits upstream and downstream of the intended barbel bait position. For some time, this tactic certainly draws the eels away from the barbel bait.

Since we can expect a bite from a barbel almost immediately a bait is placed in position after dark, it is intelligent to assume that if no bite is forthcoming after about ten minutes or so no barbel are in the swim at that time. Observation of the fish in the daytime will have confirmed their behaviour in paying periodic visits to the swim – perhaps every hour or every few minutes, the time lag varying from swim to swim. After ten minutes without a bite, therefore, there are two possible alternatives. You can either sit it out, in the knowledge that almost certainly at some time during the night the barbel will be feeding there, or you can move to a second swim, where the fish may be actively feeding at that very moment. We almost always favour the second approach, and our results over the past few seasons, which have been carefully logged, show just how effective the mobile approach is for taking multi-fish catches.

Our approach is invariably as follows. After ten minutes in the first swim without a bite a dropper of hemp is introduced before we move on to the second baited area. There the procedure is repeated, before we move on to the third swim, and so on. If a

A Thames fish ready for netting.

barbel bite is forthcoming, and a barbel successfully landed, there is little point remaining in the swim for the next half-hour or so. The best option after taking a fish is to top up the bait and then go and fish another primed area, allowing the remaining barbel to recover their composure. The swim will then be revisited later. The same comments will apply if a landed chub or eel creates an unwanted disturbance.

Six swims will be visited and revisited throughout the dark hours, perhaps each one being fished as much as ten times during a summer's night. The law of averages is such that at least some of the visits will coincide with the presence of feeding barbel, and this is confirmed by one inescapable fact. Most of the barbel that we have caught by this mobile technique have taken the bait literally seconds after it has been introduced.

It is important not to become downhearted if no action is forthcoming initially. Remember at all times the feeding behaviour of the barbel you saw in the daylight. Nothing will change after dark, and that will allow you to picture what is going on in the swims, even though you cannot see into them. Therefore you can be absolutely certain that the more times you visit a particular swim after dark without success, the closer you must be to your next visit being timed correctly. Three very big fish from the Wensum are ample proof of the technique in action. A barbel of 10lb 5oz came on the fifth visit to a swim, an 11lb 1oz fish on the eighth visit, and a 12lb 6oz specimen on no less than the tenth visit.

With this mobile approach to the fishing the time spent away from each swim, whether it has previously yielded a bite or not, is probably more important than the short time spent in it. It is important not to rush a swim. It must be left to settle for a decent interval, up to an hour, after the bait has been topped up. If about six swims are rotated in this fashion over the dark hours of a summer or autumn night, the barbel in each area will have been allowed the bulk of the dark hours to feed undisturbed. Because of this, they will be most responsive to hookbaits.

There is one very obvious exception to the above technique. Where a group of barbel have been weaned on to large quantities of maggots, a large catch can be accumulated if you remain in one swim all night. As has been stated earlier, maggot saturation results in total preoccupation and the almost entire loss of caution. When this stage is reached, despite the commotion caused by landing fish and regular topping up by either dropper or swimfeeder, barbel will remain in the area constantly, mopping up the maggots. Apart from this very special circumstance, do not fall into the trap of flogging away in one swim all night, as you will only result in undoing all the day's preparations. Not only that, you will have limited your knowledge to the one swim. You will be no further forward in establishing the potential of other areas.

There is a worthwhile refinement to the above technique, which we are using more and more. In the prebaited areas themselves, a static bait is definitely the presentation that is required. A moving bait over hemp in daylight has been seen to spook barbel badly. However, in the fast, weedy shallows, the occasional barbel will often take a moving bait, particularly around streamer weed. Obviously, the fish expect their food on the hoof, so to speak, where there is a fair current. It is useful to bear this in mind at night, for those times when the main swims are being rested. It can make a relaxing change to spend the odd twenty minutes rolling baits down the shallows, perhaps covering a great deal of water. As well as the occasional bonus barbel, a great many big chub have been taken by this entertaining little diversion, including over twenty five-pounders from the Wensum alone.

Barbel Bites at Night

Although the bites we expect from barbel are unmistakable, they do come in various forms. First we have the full-blooded wrench that comes out of nowhere. One minute the rod is lying quite still in your hand, the next it is trying to dive underwater. There is not much doubt that this indication, so beloved of barbel anglers, results from a fish picking up the bait and then suddenly becoming alarmed and bolting. There is rarely any need to strike this type of pull; the fish will normally have hooked themselves. A better kind of indication is more akin to the classic chub bite of an initial pluck and then a slow, smooth but very deliberate pull on the rod top. What a breath-taking moment that is – probably the pinnacle of excitement in barbel angling.

If you are legering upstream, or if a barbel moves upstream with your bait, which often occurs, then instead of a pull you will get a definite slack-line indication. Whilst you are more likely to experience this type of bite in very streamy water, you should be alert to the possibility of a slack-liner at all times. This is another reason why we recommend touch legering in conjunction with watching a Betalight. Relaxation of tension is very obvious to trained fingers. Similar to the slack-liner is a series of alternate reductions in tension and little bumps on the rod top. This phenomenon is caused by the barbel bumping the lead down the current. It may not have pulled the bait savagely enough to cause a true

Back she goes!

slack-liner, but this is a truly confident indication for all that.

Perhaps the most difficult indication to deal with is the fast, sudden jab, which usually occurs when a particular group of fish have undergone intense fishing pressure. The best way to overcome this problem is to fish upstream and convert the jabs to slack-liners. If, however, that is not possible, adding more lead to the terminal rig, with perhaps a reduction in length of the hooklink, will convert it to more of a bolt-rig type of arrangement. This is often enough to turn those annoying jabs into full-blooded wrenches, as the barbel hook themselves and gallop off at a rate of knots.

Preferred Feeding Times

Although the technique we have outlined is one that works throughout the dark hours, our results definitely indicate that certain times of the night are more productive than others. The dusk period and the first hour of dark is a hot time, and then sport can often slow right down until it has been dark for about four hours. We have certainly had an astonishing percentage of our big summer fish between 2 and 2.30 a.m. It is almost as if they have spent the first few hours on patrol, seeing what is about, before settling down into some serious feeding.

Provided that you can stay awake that long, the hour just before dawn is also excellent, and several big Cherwell fish have put in an appearance at this time.

The Importance of Analysis

For our approach to barbel fishing to be most effective, we like to be on the river for at least two days and nights, though three is better. The reason is that we feel that the opportunity to examine swims the day after first fishing them can yield important information. During the first day's baiting process, it is a good idea to enter on a piece of paper all relevant information about the swims you intend fishing. Such data would be amounts of baits introduced, whether any barbel were actually seen in the swim, and if so how many and how big; whether the barbel were present on every prebaiting visit you made; and how long elapsed between fish leaving and re-entering each swim. If no barbel were seen in an otherwise promising-looking swim, were other fish such as chub active over the bait? Anything that helps to build up a complete dossier of each swim is valuable.

After the night's fishing is complete, other information can be added for each swim. Where were fish landed? Where were fish seen to roll? Which swims gave bites from fish other than barbel? Which swims gave no evidence of fish activity at all? And so on. It takes very little time, but soon enable you to establish a pattern.

Let us look at one example of how such an analysis could be valuable. We may have baited six swims with equal amounts of bait during the day yet find that after dark the bulk of the activity, by both barbel and other fish, is concentrated in two of the six. This would tell us that those two areas require a greater amount of bait during the day, at more frequent intervals, to keep the barbel in the area. In this instance, heavier baiting would compensate for the presence of a large number of nuisance fish and could turn a good swim into an excellent one. Another quite devious approach, to try and keep one step ahead of the fish, can be employed where perhaps two or three fish have been taken from one swim. Experience has shown that all the remaining barbel in that swim may well be difficult to tempt the following night, but will be perfectly happy to accept a bait in a different swim. In other circumstances, heavily baiting another pitch a short distance away from the area in which the fish were caught may be a better bet than

returning to the scene of the first night's success. Again, the Wensum has shown the validity of this approach.

Some of the most valuable information can be gleaned during the first trip to each baited area the morning after the night's fishing. After a good sleep and breakfast, if there are no other anglers about, each area will have been undisturbed for several hours and may well contain feeding barbel. Again, the visual sightings for each swim can be added to all the information already gathered. You can now see how quickly the information builds up after just one day's baiting and one night's fishing. It is not difficult to understand how a whole summer spent investigating a stretch of river in this logical step-by-step sequence

An Ouse twelve-pounder goes home.

can reap tremendous rewards. Without wishing to sound immodest, the very large number of big barbel that we have taken has not resulted from luck. Our system is hard work, requiring plenty of bait, plenty of time, plenty of patience, the elimination of errors, and, above all, an absolute belief in what we are doing. We guarantee that if you adopt our technique you cannot help but catch barbel with satisfying regularity.

We would like to end this chapter by relating the story of a 10lb 14oz barbel that was taken from the Wensum, a fish that clearly demonstrates the value of observation. The first look into a swim that had yielded a couple of six-pounders the previous night revealed the presence of a very big fish just hanging motionless in mid-water, a fish that had certainly not been seen the previous day. There was plenty of bait still present, but the barbel showed no inclination to feed; it just held in the steady current. For about fifteen minutes it remained motionless in clear water above the streamer weed – highly unusual behaviour – before slowly moving upstream no more than a foot below the surface. We followed that fish for over a hundred and fifty yards before it dived down through the weed in an area that was previously thought to be shallow, with nothing to commend it as being worthy of special attention.

A session in swimming trunks soon revealed that, far from being uninteresting, the area featured a very pronounced depression and shelf – a perfect set-up which had been completely disguised by the streamer. This hitherto undiscovered retreat was baited in the normal way, and

Another lovely Cherwell double of 10lb 1oz.

an hour after dark that night a juicy lump of meat paste was accepted by the ten-pounder. It was almost as if it had led us to the spot it had wanted to be landed from! That secret little swim has since produced many barbel, and is another of those little experiences that make our fishing such a thoroughly absorbing and time-consuming addiction.

5 Fishing in Winter

UNDERSTANDING THE WEATHER

Before we discuss fishing techniques in the winter, it is necessary to understand what constitutes good weather and water conditions, and what factors affect barbel feeding behaviour at this time of the year. Only by knowing how our quarry will react to certain conditions can we adapt our approach to give us the best chance of success.

Understanding the effects on river conditions, and therefore on the barbel feeding characteristics, of our unpredictable British weather is without doubt the most important factor in consistent success with barbel during the winter months. We cannot emphasize that point too strongly. The implications of climatic changes dictate all

Definitely not ideal barbel conditions.

our decisions on where we fish, how we fish and, most important of all, when we fish.

We will demonstrate how a changing weather pattern during a fishing session totally controls events, and how the use of modern technology enables us to monitor the condition and probable change in condition of all the various barbel rivers up and down the country. At any one time we can assess the state of the Wensum in Norfolk, the rivers of Hampshire and Dorset, the Bristol Avon, and so on. More important, we can predict the influence of the weather in altering such characteristics over the coming week or so. That information allows us to be 95 per cent certain that, when we do go barbel fishing, we will find a river in such a favourable condition that success is virtually guaranteed. Obviously, we first have to know what constitutes these favourable conditions, so let us look at this vitally important aspect first.

The Importance of Temperature and Colour

There is no doubt that the two most critical factors are the water temperature and the height and clarity of the river. If we look at temperature first, there is a wealth of information that proves that the metabolic rate of all cyprinids decreases very steeply when the water temperature falls below 4°C (40°F), though there are great variations between species. Certainly, our experiences of barbel confirm that below that critical level we are really up against it. So vitally important is this question of water temperature that a thermometer is an essential item in any serious winter barbel angler's armoury. The evidence from our own fishing over many winters has been so conclusive that we would now feel that we were fishing blind if we were unable to take the water temperature.

The temperature reading when you start fishing is, however, only a small part of the story. For it to be of any benefit at all, that reading has to be coupled with others, taken regularly throughout the session, enabling a temperature gradient to be established. It is vitally important to know whether the temperature is rising or falling, and how fast, and we always take readings at least twice a day. This will be increased to three or four times daily if we have reason to suspect steep temperature changes, possibly caused by such things as persistent warm rain or overnight frosts.

Comparing readings taken during the session with information about the water and weather conditions in the days before fishing enables us to assess accurately how the barbel will respond to our bait. Let us take a simple example. A temperature reading on the first morning of fishing may be 42°F (6°C), which in isolation tells us very little. The temperature may be dropping very quickly following severe night frosts or it may be rising rapidly as the result of a cold spell having been ended by many hours of warm rain, as a milder airstream comes in. Two or three more readings throughout the day will indicate how fast the temperature is dropping or rising, or whether it is holding steady. All this information is vital, as it will determine the entire angling strategy. In certain circumstances, the evidence may be strong enough for us to make the decision that barbel fishing is not worth the effort. We can then either switch to a different species which may be more responsive or go home early to the wife and investigate other outlets for our frustration.

The ideal situation temperature is one of more than 40°F (5°C) and rising, and the faster the rate of rise the more dramatic an effect it will have on the feeding behaviour of the barbel. That is particularly true when the rise follows a period of clear, low, and very cold water, when the temperature has possibly been as low as 35°F (2°C). Such cold water induces the barbel into a forced abstinence and semi-dormant state, and the result of rapidly increasing temperature can then be to drive them into a feeding frenzy. Under these conditions, a water temperature of 42°F (6°C) and rising could be more advantageous than one of 45°F (7°C) and dropping. Any rising temperature gradient will indicate suitable barbel feeding conditions. Once over the critical 40°F (5°C), the speed of temperature rise does not seem to make that much difference. The mere fact that it is rising is sufficient. On the other hand, the speed of temperature fall is more critical. Suppose we have 45°F (7°C), and the temperature

is dropping very slowly, say 1 degree F per day. For two or three days there would be a chance of sport, as the fish gradually adjust to the slowly changing conditions. The catch rate will slowly tail off as the all important level of 40°F (5°C) is approached. However, a much more steeply falling gradient of say 3 degrees F a day will be much more detrimental and may well inhibit feeding immediately.

We have often heard, and read, that taking water temperatures is a waste of time, since there is little you can do about it and you have to make the best of what you have on the day of fishing. Some of our friends have made that statement. With the greatest respect to them, we are adamant that that is a very shortsighted viewpoint. An

Midnight in November – spicy meat – 10lb 4oz

understanding of how temperature controls feeding behaviour will help you to catch fish that might otherwise not be taken. Let us just take one simple example from our own fishing.

Four winters ago, on the Royalty, we were faced with a river apparently perfect for very mobile fishing with meat baits. On the first morning we recorded a temperature of 44°F (6°C), and as the water was also nicely coloured and the weather overcast and mild, we could hardly have wished for better. Although we caught a barbel each early that first day, the action was not as fast and furious as we would have expected, and we were surprised to record a temperature of only 42°F (6°C) in the evening. There was no apparent reason for the drop that we could ascertain at the time, though we found out later that there had been quite a severe frost only a few miles inland. Obviously, this had led to an influx of colder water downstream several hours later. The next morning the temperature was down to 40°F (5°C), though visually the river still appeared perfect. That further 2-degree drop told us that mobile fishing would probably be non-productive and we switched to static fishing with the feeder and maggots, an approach we felt the conditions demanded. This led us to take several nice fish, including a fat nine-pounder. Other anglers, misreading the conditions, persevered with the mobile approach and caught nothing. This story is not to show how clever we are. It merely demonstrates how the information given to us by the thermometer was used to help us make the right decision on the day, and catch a few fish that would not otherwise have been caught. Our barbel fishing over many winters contains dozens of such examples.

If we have laboured the question of temperature, it has been quite deliberate. We cannot over emphasize the importance we place on the thermometer, and recom-

mend that you acquire one before your next barbel-fishing expedition. Learn how to interpret the information it provides, and how to adapt your fishing technique in response to temperature changes. If you follow this simple piece of advice, we guarantee that your catches will improve as a result.

If the temperature and temperature gradient are favourable, therefore, we know that the barbel will feed, and this will be true whatever the clarity of the water. However, clear water conditions give us the same problems as we face in the summer, with barbel spooking at the sight of large baits in the day. It is once again advisable to present particles during the hours of daylight and the larger meat-based offerings after dark. It is a matter of adapting your approach to suit the prevailing conditions.

If we have a coloured river, however, with favourable temperatures, then we have the optimum conditions of all for barbel angling. It is not difficult to see why. One of the main reasons for increasing colour in the river will be the inflow of warm rain, which not only provides the upward temperature gradient that is so important but also gives the fish low light intensity in which to feed more confidently. Be aware, though, that increasing colour is also caused by melting snow water, which will lead to falling temperatures and also, with almost all our rivers these days, temporary deoxygenation if road salt is being carried. Just because you find a good colour, therefore, do not be misled into thinking that you can safely leave the thermometer in your car.

Teletext and Telephone

The arrival of the Teletext service has revolutionized our barbel angling. Advance weather forecasting is now so accurate in

A fine double from the Bristol Avon – 11lb 10oz.

predicting overall climatic changes, and when they are likely to occur, that blank days are virtually a thing of the past. We fish only when the odds are heavily stacked in our favour. It is interesting to see how we apply this principle individually. Trefor is a barbel-only angler, with little interest in any other species at the moment. His working life is therefore arranged so that when the water conditions are favourable he can go barbel fishing for several days to take full advantage of them. The thirty-eight double-figure barbel that he has caught over the last few seasons have not resulted from the odd lucky session but from careful planning.

Tony, whose working life is slightly more rigid, uses the same information in a slightly different way. If you are an all-rounder, establishing which conditions favour which fish make it easy to assess what species to go for on any particular session. During the wildly fluctuating weather patterns of January and February 1990 this principle resulted in the capture of barbel to over nine pounds, roach to over two pounds, chub to over five pounds and pike to over twenty pounds – surely an indication that considerably more than luck is involved.

Let us take an imaginary Teletext weather forecast and see how we make use of it, in conjunction with any other information to hand. Let us assume that there has been a period of high pressure over the country, with sunny days and frosty nights. There has been little rain anywhere for about two weeks, and the weather map shows that, while night temperatures are hovering around freezing point in

Hampshire, they are dropping to as low as 27°F (–2°C) in Norfolk. Telephone calls to various friends, tackle shops and water authorities have confirmed that all our favourite barbel rivers are running at normal winter height and clarity, with the exception of the Wensum, which is below average level, clear and very cold. The only cloud cover is concentrated in the Midlands, where the night temperatures are two or three degrees above zero.

Suppose that this particular weather pattern is forecast to remain unchanged for several days. We can see straight away that conditions are not likely to be good for barbel fishing, and chub or pike are certainly a better bet. If, however, you insist on fishing for barbel, the Midland rivers such as the Thames or the Kennet are likely to be more productive than the Hampshire Avon, and they would probably only be really responsive after dark to large baits, as there will be little colour. Water temperature is unlikely to be brilliant, but there will be a chance of the odd fish picking up a bait.

The Teletext may reveal, however, that an intense low pressure front is approaching the south-west of the country, carrying heavy and sustained rain with it, and is due to make its presence felt in the Bristol area in two days' time. We can see from the chart that fresh-to-strong winds are predicted, with night temperatures dropping to a minimum of 46°F (8°C). The speed of movement of the frontal system means that it will take a day to spread along the south coast, and a further day before it enters East Anglia. At about the same time, the rain will be clearing up in the south-west, again being replaced by another settled spell of high pressure. How can all this information be interpreted to best effect?

First of all, the Bristol Avon will be showing the first visible reaction to the rain, in the form of rising level and increasing colour, about twenty-four hours after it starts to fall, though the impact on raising the water temperature will occur much sooner. The first surge of high water will bring accumulated debris into the river, whereafter it will be in perfect trim for barbel to feed ravenously. Our trip will therefore be timed for three days' time, to coincide with those perfect conditions. There will then be a further two days of high water and favourable water temperatures, before the river starts to fine off and the temperature gradually drops back as the high pressure moves in. That will be the signal to leave; the best of the fishing will be over. But look what is happening elsewhere. As conditions on the Bristol Avon are deteriorating, the Hampshire Avon and Dorset Stour are reaching perfection, as are the Midland rivers, and a further two days on any of those could pay handsome dividends.

Last of all, we have the Wensum. At the start of the weather system, it offered the worst prospects. Now it offers potentially the best. Because it was exceptionally low, clear and cold, the effect of the heavy rain in Norfolk will see the most rapidly rising temperature gradient of all, and the barbel will respond with frenzied feeding.

From the above, it is easy to see how we could map out a week's barbel fishing to correspond with optimum conditions in different areas of the country, by simply sitting at home, studying the weather map and making the odd phone call.

Let us close this very important section with a couple of real-life examples to reinforce the points we have made.

In February 1990, the Six O'clock News showed the Severn and Thames catchment areas to be an inland sea, with homes and offices under several feet of brown, swirling floodwater. Trefor and Mick Nicholls's planned trip to the Bristol Avon would have to be aborted. A challenge is one

What a brace – 22lb 8oz of barbel!

thing, but it does help if you know where the river is. At the same time, it was assessed that, provided there was no further substantial rain, the river would be back within its banks, and perhaps running about two feet above normal, by the following Tuesday evening. Conditions would then be perfect.

Careful monitoring of the weather maps confirmed that the water was likely to be receding as assumed, and so the trip went ahead as planned, for a four-day session. Two hours after they left Coventry Trefor and Mick found the river exactly as predicted, two feet up, well coloured and with a temperature of 46°F (8°C). Success was guaranteed, and when the first session finally ended at 3a.m., Mick had netted barbel of 4lb 6oz, 7lb 4oz, 8lb 8oz and 9lb

7oz, and Trefor had chipped in with a super brace of 8lb 8oz and 9lb 1oz. The prospects for the rest of the stay looked brilliant.

The next day, they were up and about at the crack of midday, and moved down river to a stretch that offered a better chance of a really big fish. With the swim preparation complete, they were confident that exciting barbel action lay ahead again, and, indeed, that second session saw another nine barbel landed, with the top fish of 10lb 2oz to Mick. That second day and night, however, was characterized by the return of very much stronger winds, and the rain grew steadily heavier and more persistent. By the following morning, with the rain still lashing down on the van roof, they feared the worst and, sure enough, a quick observation showed that there had been a further two-foot rise in level while they slept. As the rain still hammered down, conditions were deteriorating fast, tons of floating debris and turbid muddy boils giving the river an angry and inhospitable look. It was time for a rethink.

The problem had several possible solutions. The first was to move across country to the Stour or Hampshire Avon. It was known that these rivers were both running bank-high at the start of the trip and, as the rain was tracking east anyway, the conditions would similarly worsen on those two rivers also. That possibility was therefore discounted. The Wensum was the next consideration, but it too was discounted. It was at least five hours' drive away, involving heavy expense in fuel costs, and, although it held plenty of water, having received the tail end of the storms, it was known that temperatures were several degrees colder than in the west. Again, there were too many negatives.

A stronger possibility was the Thames, which was full to the brim but certainly fishable, and in the prevailing conditions could well produce the kind of barbel that dreams are made of. Again, though, it would not take the influx of too much more water to make the Thames burst its banks. The Kennet provided the perfect solution. The catchment area below Newbury is a vast chalk reserve, able to absorb enormous amounts of rainfall before it starts to spill over into the river. The Kennet holds its water like no other river we know. The Thames, Severn, Teme, Cherwell and Bristol Avon can all be raging torrents, yet the Kennet can be in perfect barbel trim, with good colour and fast smooth glides.

Accordingly, Mick and Trefor headed for a prolific stretch of the Kennet, involving a forty-mile drive, and their assumptions were found to be spot on. The conditions were indeed excellent for winter barbel, and a further thirty-one fish to over eight pounds graced their landing nets in the two days and nights that remained.

In January, 1990, Tony arrived on the Dorset Stour for a three-day session, and was pleased to find the river as expected, high and coloured. The temperature, at 42°F (6°C) was not quite as high as would have been ideal, but prospects were nevertheless reasonable to good. The first night's fishing on a very difficult stretch of river never produced a barbel, though conditions looked excellent, but the capture of several eels demonstrated that the barbel would certainly be feeding if they had been located. Throughout the following day, the promised misty conditions with steady light rain never materialized, as the weather front moved across the country much further north than expected. Instead, the sky was clear and blue, and the continuing strong wind turning decidedly chilly. That evening, the water temperature had shown a drop of 1°F, and again only eels and a solitary chub were caught.

The last morning dawned bright and clear, with a good frost in evidence, and one look at the river showed it to have cleared rapidly in the night and lost about 8in (20cm) in height. The prospects were worsening by the hour, and a phone call home confirmed that rain was now pouring down in the Midlands, and had been for the last eighteen hours. That was all Tony needed to know. Three hours later, he was baiting swims on the Cherwell, which were now in perfect trim, and that evening six barbel were landed in quick succession, a catch that included two eight-pounders and two nine-pounders.

The above examples demonstrate that the good fish which were caught were not a result of luck or guesswork. The decisions that we had taken rationally had allowed us to be at the right place at the right time.

The changing conditions at the first venue could have curtailed the fishing prematurely, had not we had access to knowledge about conditions elsewhere.

Other anglers often tell us we have been lucky in finding the river in such good condition. Luck has nothing to do with it. Conscious decisions put us there at the right time. Understanding the weather, and its effects on the water, is fundamental to our barbel fishing. Without that understanding we could never hope to achieve the level of consistency with our barbel catching that we enjoy and which you will certainly achieve also if you are prepared to follow our advice. We can do no more than guarantee that if you take the trouble to chart the changing weather patterns, and learn to asess how they will affect the barbel's feeding behaviour, you will soon find that blank days are things that happen to other anglers.

WINTER ANGLING METHODS

Fishing Techniques for Ideal Conditions

We have arrived on the banks of our favourite fishery to find a river 18in (45cm) above normal winter level and carrying a nice rich tea colour, with a temperature of 46°F (8°C). As it has been mild and damp for several days, we can be fairly certain that the temperatue reading should be either stable or possibly rising slowly. Before we even start fishing, our confidence is now sky-high. We know that every barbel in the river will be feeding hard. It is just a matter of finding them.

This confidence and attitude of mind is very important. If you believe that every barbel in the river is feeding, then you must

Difficult barbel conditions on the Cherwell.

A February barbel from Throop.

also believe that if you are not having bites in a swim, it is for one of two reasons only. Either you have spooked the fish by a clumsy presentation or the fish are not there. This belief determines our entire angling strategy in good winter conditions, as it does throughout the warmer summer months. The keyword is mobility.

After prebaiting all the areas we intend searching, as described in Chapter 3, it is time to begin a systematic tracking down of the barbel. Initially, the object is to locate swims containing fish, either by catching one or seeing them roll. Rolling fish are feeding fish, of that there can be no doubt, and a bait dropped adjacent to the position of a roll will usually result in a bite in seconds. We remember well a 10lb 10oz Wensum fish. Trefor was fishing a well-known

gravel slope, a feature that has produced many big fish for us. Across the river, over a thick weedbed, a big barbel rolled. Without hesitation, the bait was retrieved and cast to land where the fish had just broken surface. Within seconds there was a firm pull on the rod tip, and another Wensum double was fighting a losing battle for its freedom.

Daytime fishing is therefore very much a search-and-locate procedure, eliminating unproductive areas and isolating those few swims that will be prepared for after dark – which, as in summer, is by far the best time to catch barbel. When the swims have been found, it is important that they are not flogged to death in the day. It is preferable to adopt the same tactics as in a summer night, fishing for very short periods and keeping the feed topped up regularly. The object is to have as many known barbel-holding areas primed for after-dark fishing as possible, and with them all containing fish that have undergone the minimum of disturbance during the day.

This approach is far superior to more static methods when conditions are known to be good, not least for encouraging positive bites. The one thing that leads to tentative barbel bites is for the fish to be consistently hammered in one area. Our view is that it is pointless to flog away all day in one swim for perhaps two fish while spooking all the other residents in the process. Those same two fish will still be caught by the mobile approach, the difference being that several other swims would have been investigated at the same time, giving the first one ample and frequent rest periods. If swims are carefully nursed, it is not unusual for us to take two

barbel from two casts, in several different spots, on a winter's night.

As potential barbel-holding areas are more extensive in the winter, because of increased water depth and much-reduced vegetation, it is vital that the searching tactics on any baited section are thorough, with the hookbait probing the entire area. The diagram shows an example of a typical winter glide, the kind of swim that certainly provides the bulk of our winter action. The uniform glide has been baited with hemp and corn in various positions – near bank, far bank and midstream. The swim is some forty yards long, and the task is to search that entire area as comprehensively as possible, at the same time causing the minimum disturbance. Let us examine the bait-presentation possibilities.

There is no doubt that the normal approach would be to position yourself at A,

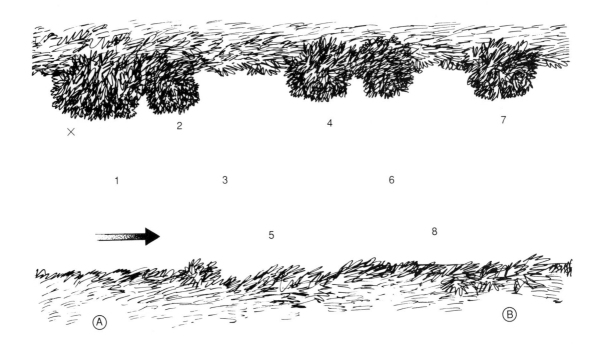

A typical winter glide.

at the upstream extremity of the glide. From that position, a downstream-and-across presentation would be in operation. There is nothing at all wrong with that in a known swim, but for searching a long glide it has inherent weaknesses. Suppose you have cast across to swim number 2. After a few minutes, no bite has materialized and the rod point is lifted to dislodge the lead, which then rolls into midstream in an arc, before settling to fish swim number 3. The same procedure is subsequently followed to manoeuvre the bait to swim number 5. While this approach is undoubtedly less alarming than making individual casts to the three swims specified, it does entail a bait moving across the flow on a tight line, which is both unnatural and prone to increase the risk of line bites.

From the above, it can be seen that if the cast is lengthened to swim 4, another arc can be covered to fish swims 6 and 8 in the same way, and so on down the run. The problems with the technique, in the context of searching a long glide, are threefold. First, the swim can be searched only in a series of arcs across the current, which is totally unnatural. In a strong flow, food items simply do not behave in that fashion. Second, to cover the available water thoroughly, a multitude of casts are required, which will be potentially highly alarming to the fish. Third, and as a direct result of the second drawback, this bombardment of the glide with lead can result in nervous bites. We have always said that most barbel bites are unmissable, and still stick to that as a general rule. However, there is no getting away from the fact that, on a river where the barbel are being constantly pursued, many bites deteriorate into fast jabs.

For many years, we adopted exactly the procedure outlined above, and certainly caught plenty of barbel in the process. However, we now know that we were only scratching the surface of the potential that is available from a far superior approach, which we shall now offer as an alternative.

Consider fishing the swim seated at position B, so that each prebaited area is fished upstream and across. We will go into the mechanics of the technique a little later, but let us first examine the principles involved, and understand the fundamental differences in presentation from the downstream method just discussed. Once again, a cast has been made to swim number 2, now obviously upstream and across. After the same few minutes biteless, it is now time to begin the searching process, and once more we shift the lead to fish a different position. This time, however, there is no unnatural arcing of the terminal tackle across the current. If the line is gently drawn, the lead shifts and then bumps down the flow in a straight line. Because we are fishing upstream, dislodging the lead creates slack line at the rod, and so nothing prevents the bait from making a natural progression downstream, following the current. This is critically important. The movements of the lead by hand manipulation of the line can be as delicate as you wish, and you can cover literally every inch of a run – along a straight line, obviously – with just one cast. The implications are obvious. The single cast minimizes the disturbance and if, in fact, the cast is made above the first baited area, marked X on the diagram, the whole run can be fished as thoroughly as you like, without once actually casting to a spot where you expect a barbel to be. It is difficult to envisage a less alarming presentation than that. Obviously, many different lines of presentation could be fished in the same way, and in our example, two more casts would suffice – one for the midstream area and one for the near bank run, in each case the cast being made above the first baited area.

In all our years of big-fish angling, other

anglers we have seen upstream legering in this fashion could be counted on the fingers of one hand, yet it is one of the deadliest methods we know. So let us have a look at how we go about it in practice.

The first thing we have to get right is the terminal rig, and our standard set up is shown in the diagram. One of the most important features is the snap link swivel, since the ability to change leads quickly and efficiently according to the demands of individual swims is vital. Indeed, some swims may require a different lead at different points along their length. The weight is critical if you are to fish upstream efficiently. It must obviously be heavy enough to hold bottom against the prevailing current, and yet not so heavy that a gentle pull with the fingers will not dislodge it. Once dislodged, it should settle

again quickly as soon as the line is released. The quivertip is an essential tool in judging the correct weight for the job. We invariably use 3oz Drennan tips in the winter, and the weight is about right when the tip will accept about a 4-inch upstream deflection before dislodging the lead. This supposes a reasonably brisk current, when the technique is at its most effective. If the current is very sluggish, it is better to work with lighter leads, providing that the casting weight is adequate, and a smaller tip deflection.

Having placed the first cast in position, allow the bait to settle and the tip to bend to its required deflection, so that the tackle is now perfectly balanced. After perhaps two minutes, draw a little line gently with the left hand, not forgetting to take the resulting slack onto the reel. The lead moves

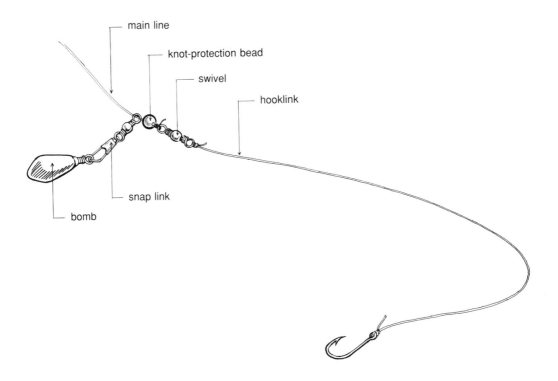

main line

knot-protection bead

swivel

hooklink

snap link

bomb

Our standard terminal rig set up.

perhaps two feet downstream, where it again settles. The procedure is repeated until the entire run has been covered. The movement of the disturbed lead is quite characteristic: it usually gives two slow bounces to move two feet, if the tackle is correctly balanced, before coming to rest again. As this is happening, the tip movement is correspondingly slow: it eases backwards and forwards gently as the terminal rig repositions itself. Very rarely, with the notable exception of the Royalty, do we get bites actually as the lead is moving, but the minute after it settles is very reliable. As we have said before, the conditions we are discussing are ones we consider perfect. Remember, all the barbel will be feeding, and, if a bait enters their field of vision naturally, they will have it at once. If there is no bite within another two minutes, therefore, we assume that no barbel are there and move the lead again to continue the search.

The bites take several forms. Very rarely do you get savage pulls, unless you are fishing in a very sluggish current or using an excessively heavy lead. The bite normally consists of a very definite kick back of the quivertip, as the line falls slack, caused by the barbel moving downstream with the bait and dislodging the lead. A more leisurely barbel pick-up will move the lead by small amounts; this usually occurs only moments after the tackle has settled after a manual movement. What happens is that when the bait settles in front of a fish it moves forwards and mouths it. It has no reason to be suspicious, and very slowly moves down with it. The usual indication this gives is a much sharper bounce of the lead, with possibly two or three quick bounces happening in seconds. A succession of small rapid kicks back of the tip will occur simultaneously. This is a very confident bite, and should be struck immediately. Let us look at the sequence of events

again, as it is very important to recognize this most common indication of an upstream bite. We have two slow bounces of the lead as we move it, and then it settles. Seconds later, there are two or three very quick bounces and relaxations of tension. Strike!

Knowing that sequence will also allow you to recognize other possible bites. For instance, if you have shifted the lead manually, and it does not bounce when it should, there is a good chance that the reason is that a barbel has the bait in its mouth. The first barbel that Tony ever caught from the Bristol Avon gave a bite of this type. The second time the lead was moved, instead of resettling as it should have done it continued moving downstream. When the slack had been retrieved the strike was made into a very surprised seven-pounder. To sum up, then, strike if the lead does something it should not do, or fails to do something it should.

This upstream searching technique is undoubtedly at its best when used in reasonably streamy water, as you can utilize the current to aid the presentation, maintain the tautness in the line, and show up slack-line bites very obviously. But the method can also be applied when the flow is much more sedate, though you may actually have to pull the bait downstream in the absence of sufficient flow to do the job for you. Pulling the bait, as opposed to tweaking the lead and letting the current do the work, is not quite so efficient, as it leads to a little arcing of the terminal rig towards midstream, and there is little you can do about it. More casts per swim will be required because of this than where the flow is brisker. When fishing upstream in this manner, so convinced are we that few presentations offer such a low scare factor that we often walk backwards down the bank, to cover as long a run as possible from a single cast. If you are doing this, however,

Another Bristol Avon belter – this one weighed in at 11lb 10oz.

be careful not to walk into the river, thus disturbing the near-bank baited area.

There is another vitally important point to make about why upstream legering is such an effective search technique for establishing likely feeding areas. A bait that is periodically allowed to trundle downstream will automatically locate obstructions such as the roots of dead weedbeds or rises in the gravel, exactly the kind of feature where barbel might be expected to lurk. These features will be undetectable visually in the winter. If you know the river well from fishing it in summer, you will have an idea where the weedbeds are, but the technique will allow you to locate them with precise accuracy. In that way you have

an enormous advantage, in being able to fish swims that most other anglers are not aware even exist.

As in the summer, daylight winter fishing is merely a preamble to the more serious stuff after dark, its main purpose being to isolate perhaps half a dozen swims to be fished in rotation. Once again, the secret at night is keeping on the move; there is no point remaining in a swim if no bites are forthcoming. The chances are that the swim is barren of barbel at that time. Introduce the bait naturally and inconspicuously and, wherever possible, use the upstream presentation, especially for any swim in mid-river or at the far bank, where there is no alternative but to cast a heavy lead. As in daylight, cast above the baited area and manoeuvre the terminal rig into the correct position manually. For near-bank runs, where the bait can be lowered into place very accurately without any disturbance, a normal downstream presentation is perfectly acceptable. However, if your barbel give tentative bites switch to the upstream presentation for near-bank swims also.

Taking the trouble to minimize the disturbance caused when introducing the hookbait is just as important when the river is high and coloured in winter as it was when it was low and clear on a balmy July night. Just because you cannot see the fish does not mean they will not be as alarmed by splashy casting.

An essential part of all our barbel fishing, but particularly in winter, when stronger currents enforce the use of more weight and cause much more tautness in the tackle, is combining visual bite indication with touch legering. With practice, your fingers can convey a wealth of information about what is going on at the business end, and nowhere is it more valuable than in upstream legering after dark. As we have seen, the success of the method lies in identifying many varied slack-line indications, many of which would be impossible to detect at night by relying on a Betalight on the quivertip alone. If you have set a 3in (7.5cm) upstream deflection into the tip, which straightens suddenly, all that tells you is that the lead has moved at least 3in (7.5cm). It does not tell you whether it has resettled, how much farther it has moved, or whether it is still moving. Nor does it tell you whether the lead is bouncing or not – in fact, you have not got a clue what is happening. Remember, you cannot actually see the angle or movement of the line as you obviously can in daylight. We cannot recommend too strongly that you persevere with the use of your fingers to back up whatever visual indicator you prefer. If you adopt this approach in the daytime as well, you will be able to relate all the indications you can see with the corresponding sensation of the line on your fingers, and this will prove invaluable in identifying the various signals you might experience at night.

Two recent double-figure fish to Trefor were both caught in identical circumstances, and strongly reinforce the above point. On the Wensum, a 10lb 10oz fish picked up a meat paste bait and a heavy lead and swam downstream with them, in obviously confident manner. It held the bait so high in the water that the lead did not bounce, and the corresponding sensation on the fingers was a sudden loss of tension. Not only that, there was no further sensation whatever; it was as if the line had been cut and a rod only was being held. Obviously, the line was falling downstream very rapidly indeed, and it was the work of an instant to take up the slack and strike the hook into a highly indignant barbel. A repeat performance on the Bristol Avon last season led to the landing of a personal best for the river of 11lb 10oz.

Fishing in Normal Winter Conditions

Provided that the water temperature and the temperature trend are satisfactory, barbel will feed actively no matter what the clarity of the river, and what follows is concerned with conditions when the river is at normal height and the water either clear or, at most, that bottle-green colour so indicative of good chub fishing.

The first thing to say is that the night-fishing approach will be exactly the same as described above. Generally speaking, the lack of substantial colour will correspond with lower levels and lesser flows, and this will naturally determine the actual swims

This fish fought like a wildcat in a winter flood.

prebaited and the terminal-rig weight. That apart, the swims selected are fished in rotation as before.

It is during the daylight hours that a different strategy is called for. As in clearer water at all times, our experience shows that large meat-based baits are taboo, and particle-bait fishing has been a far superior presentation. Over the last few winters, many barbel have fallen to tares, sweetcorn, casters and, on one memorable occasion on the Stour, black hemp mini-boilies. There is no doubt, however, that the particle-fishing approach to beat them all in the winter is the block-end swimfeeder coupled with large quantities of maggots. That method can be devastatingly effective, but it is imperative that enough maggots are used. Swimfeeders are at best very clumsy appendages, and very difficult to cast delicately, especially if you are fishing a streamy run requiring a heavily weighted feeder. To compensate for the alarm swimfeeders must undoubtedly cause the barbel if they are refilled and recast often enough, the fish will eventually associate the splash with feeding time. Once that situation has been reached, which can take a couple of hours, bites will often occur only seconds after the feeder has settled. In favourable water temperatures, we would not dream of embarking on a days block-ending without at least half a gallon of maggots, and a gallon is better. We will recast a large feeder every five minutes or so, and this is one situation in which you can literally buy your fish. The more maggots you can afford to use, the greater the potential for a good catch of fish. This was certainly the case on the Dorset Stour in the last week of the 1987/88 season, when nearly a gallon and a half of bait in a crease-type swim resulted in a terrific haul of eleven barbel, averaging over 6½lb, with the best two scaling 8lb 2oz and 8lb 6oz.

Obviously, to be at its most effective,

feeder fishing is essentially static fishing, steadily building up a selected glide with bait throughout the day. If you intend to fish after dark, therefore, regular breaks from the fishing to prebait a few areas are important if you are going to get the best from the night fishing. The first swim to try after dark is, however, the one which has received the volume of maggots in the day. As soon as the light fades, whilst they will still obviously accept maggots, the barbel will attack large meaty baits with great savagery, and it is not uncommon to take several fish in quick succession on meat-based baits at night from a swim which has been prebaited with maggots all day.

There is nothing wrong in continuing the feeder approach after dark in the same swim, if static fishing is your preference, but it certainly becomes less effective. A regular stream of maggots drifting down the current is an extremely attractive visual stimulant to the barbel but clearly much of that impact is lost at night, when the barbel cannot rely on sight to find their food, and have to revert to their senses of smell and touch. If you are going to use maggots after dark, therefore, a large bunch of up to fifteen on a size 6 hook is likely to be more productive than the more normal daytime approach of two or three on a size 12.

It is also advisable to use a bunch of maggots on a largish hook when fishing in snaggy areas, so that maximum pressure can be applied to a powerful fish should it need to be held out of danger. Fifteen maggots on a size 6 Au Lion d'Or may look all wrong, but it works! Several recent catches from the Cherwell have confirmed that fact. In January 1990, six fish were taken in a few hours from one swim into which nearly a gallon of bait had been introduced. All the barbel were hooked only feet away from alder roots and had to be held hard and, as the catch included two eight-pounders and two fish of 9lb 6oz and

9lb 9oz, the security of the large hook was absolutely essential.

Daytime fishing with the feeder is the one approach in which naturally moving bait can be so effective. As we have just said, the barbel become very turned on by the sight of many maggots wafting down the current at all levels, and will flash and dart to intercept as many as possible. With a hooklink of about 3ft (1m) two or three maggots on a small hook will behave much as the unfettered maggots, especially in streamy water.

It is vitally important to ensure the correct presentation for any given swim. The maggots must all be introduced along the same line to get the best from the baiting technique, and the feeder cannot therefore be allowed to roll all over the river, scattering bait far and wide. That is worse than useless, and will result in more barbel being encouraged out of the swim than are encouraged into it. So the feeder must be weighted adequately, so that it stays where it is cast. If the current demands it, we use those flattened feeders, which hold bottom more efficiently, and if necessary have no compunction in fitting them with additional weight in the form of those clip-on leads known either as ski or sledge leads.

There is one particularly fascinating aspect of feeder fishing which overcomes one of the greatest drawbacks of the method, that of the disturbance created during casting. That is to fish upstream, exactly as for the previously described searching technique. If you cast up and across, the feeder can be landed upstream of the position required, and then eased downstream to fish the correct spot. Because, as we have seen, the feeder will move down in a straight line when it is dislodged, any maggots escaping will still follow the correct baiting line. Believe us when we tell you that this is an absolutely deadly method of fishing the block-end

Winter eight-pounder from the Royalty.

78

swimfeeder, and large catches can result if you practise the technique. Bites are exactly as described earlier, provided that you have gone to the trouble of matching the correct weight of feeder to the swim in question. We have both had tremendous catches of barbel from both the Severn and the Royalty to this upstream-feeder technique, when not a single pull on the quivertip has occurred. The only indication has been a bounce as the feeder became dislodged, giving all the time in the world to strike.

If you do not want to be confined to static fishing with the block-end feeder, and prefer a mobile approach, even though the conditions are too clear for the more traditional large barbel baits, such as luncheon meat, during the day, you can fish with bread baits for chub with a real possibility of picking up bonus barbel by so doing. Bread flake and bread crust are barbel baits that should certainly not be discounted, and numerous fish from the Stour, Hampshire Avon, Wensum and Kennet are testimony to its effectiveness. Under the conditions we are discussing here, bread baits will certainly not take as many barbel as the block-end feeder, but it is another alternative to keep in mind when you fancy a change. Bread is fished exactly as in chub fishing, with a tail length of about 18in (45cm) for flake and 2 or 3in (5–7.5cm) for legered crust. From the Dorset Stour and Wensum in particular, many five-pound chub have come along to our barbel baits, and at that size are welcome intruders at any time.

Finally, in clear water as in coloured, good old lobworms are always worth a try. They will take their share of barbel under all conditions, day or night, and we never venture on to any barbel river without a few lobs in our tackle box. Their drawback, in winter as in summer, is that eels love them.

Fishing in Low, Clear and Cold Conditions

These are undoubtedly the most unproductive conditions of all for barbel fishing. Clear, bright days, crystal-clear water and temperatures plummeting well below zero at night all add up to the most daunting prospect for the barbel angler. The best advice we can offer is not to bother. You are far better employed fishing for pike or chub. If, however, you insist on trying, the only worthwhile method is to use the swimfeeder, fishing a very still bait in a known swim, and baiting very sparingly. These are not conditions when the barbel will devour pints of maggots. The best you can hope for is that an occasional fish will pick a bait up, and one or two maggots on a small hook is about the only method with any chance of success. A pint of maggots would be more than adequate for a whole day's fishing under these conditions, casting once every hour at most. One important point: you will find that you have to open out the holes in your feeder if you are to fish in this style in very cold water. The maggots become very comatose and refuse to wriggle, and have to be washed out of the feeder rather than crawling out.

The last time we fished for barbel under these conditions was about five years ago on the Royalty. On the last day of a three-day trip, we knew we were up against it. There had been three successive night frosts, which had seen the temperature plummet and the river lose all vestige of colour. Despite that, we stubbornly decided to give it a go, and fished side by side in the swim above the pipe bridge, under the marginal trees. A bitterly cold, biting east wind and periodic snow showers made our ears tingle. Despite that, we actually had one bite each, hooking two very big barbel indeed. Sadly, both fish eventually managed to shed the tiny hook, and as they

Tony with a cracking 9lb 2oz Bristol Avon fish.

were both well over nine pounds that was very disappointing. What a brace that would have made for a photograph, with snow in the background!

As far as night fishing in these conditions is concerned, if you want to be on a river at night when the frosty grass crackles underneath your feet, the landing net freezes to the ground, the line freezes in the rings, and your ears are blue with ten degrees of frost, then good luck to you! That is not our idea of fun.

Temperature Conversion Chart

Centigrade	Fahrenheit	Centigrade	Fahrenheit
0	32.0	11	51.8
1	33.8	12	53.6
2	35.6	13	55.4
3	37.4	14	57.2
4	39.2	15	59.0
5	41.0	16	60.8
6	42.8	17	62.6
7	44.6	18	64.4
8	46.4	19	66.2
9	48.2	20	68.0
10	50.0	21	69.8

A streamlined winter barbel.

CONCLUSION

We have seen that success with winter barbel is so very dependent on prevailing conditions. Moreover, catching them is very much an attitude of mind. You really must believe that the baiting, searching and fishing techniques will ensure long-term success. Confidence in what you are doing is often a very underrated factor, and we always like to look for positive signals, especially when things are not going too well. For example, our adrenalin always gets a tremendous boost when warm rain starts, or we can see yesterday's rain beginning to colour the river. Similarly, we fish with a new determination when cloud cover comes in to lower the light intensity. We always believe that these changes in conditions persuade the fish to begin feeding.

Whether that is true or not is often irrelevant. The fact that we believe it to be true is sufficient to encourage us to more determined effort, which, more often than not, brings its own reward. Anything that acts as a confidence booster is to be welcomed.

On the same topic, it is also important to be aware of negative factors. If you have enjoyed two days of good fishing in perfect conditions, but you can now see a falling, clearing river, the sky is clear and sunny with the promise of a frost to come, and the wind has veered to the north or east, then you would be wise to consider whether to curtail your barbel fishing early. Valuable barbel-fishing time is best spent when conditions are stacked heavily in your favour, not against you. Above all, remember that barbel, unlike some fish, respond well to systematic, intelligent angling. Keep your eyes open, your brain active, and you cannot fail.

6 A Month on the Cherwell

Tony Miles

Of all the barbel fishing I have done in over thirty years the most memorable to date has to be the four weeks spent on the banks of the Cherwell in September and October 1989. The fish I caught in that period, from my favourite river and one in which the barbel potential had never been seriously examined, exceeded my wildest expectations, and have led me to the firm belief that the river could well hold an as yet undiscovered specimen to shake the national barbel record.

We have to go back five years to trace the real beginnings of my serious involvement with the river as a viable barbel fishery. I

The start of an era – a 6lb 1oz Cherwell barbel.

took my first, a modest sample of just over six pounds, in the summer of 1984, and followed this up with a few others to just under eight pounds in the three seasons that followed. Those early sorties saw me lose no fewer than four possible double-figure fish, all from the same area, and all very probably the same fish. I never was to land that barbel. The area became very well known to local children, and from then on serious and peaceful fishing was impossible.

At the time I knew of only three areas where barbel could be found on the Cherwell, and all of them were now extremely well known and very hard fished. I decided that my only alternative was to find some new fish for myself, if possible in an area that received little attention from big-fish anglers and one in which I could try some new ideas.

The barbel potential on the Cherwell was really an unknown quantity. The few anglers who had made contact with one of those bewhiskered battlers had taken fish up to about nine pounds in the main, though the fish I had lost had twice been out to friends at just over ten pounds. The biggest barbel known to have come from the river was one of just over eleven pounds many years previously, but that fish had never been seriously threatened since.

In the summer of 1987 I arrived at a new stretch of river, one which I knew from chub fishing many years previously. I had remembered seeing a small barbel there over fifteen years before, though I had only ever seen the one fish. It would do for a start, though. If only that one fish were still present, it would now be very worth catching.

My very first reconnaissance trip changed the entire course of my barbel fishing. I had been on the bank only ten minutes, on a lovely bright July morning, when I spotted four barbel together, over a clear gravel run behind thick streamer. They were all good fish of seven pounds plus, and the biggest was a belter, possibly as big as eleven pounds. I had found what I was looking for.

After several weeks of fishing for those barbel without any success whatever, I was eliminating all the mistakes in my presentation, and that finally paid off handsomely in September of that year, when I took four fish in quick succession one afternoon on lobworms. The biggest of those barbel weighed 10lb 3oz, a fish I still rate as one of my most memorable captures. The feeling I experienced that day is difficult to describe. It was one of total euphoria.

I was to get a real shock on the very next trip. I had only ever seen one really big fish in the new stretch, which I had caught, and was firmly convinced that was the biggest barbel in residence. Most of the other fish seemed to be around the same size, between six and possibly eight pounds, and after landing the ten-pounder, I was already contemplating moving on. Looking back on it now, with the benefit of hindsight, that would have been a stupidly premature thing to do. Luckily, another big fish put in an appearance at exactly the right time. I had returned to the scene of my previous week's triumph to see if I could tempt the only one of the shoal of

fish that I had not caught. There had been five barbel feeding over my hemp, and I had taken four of them. The one that had evaded me weighed possibly nine pounds.

As I peered over the marginal rushes on my arrival in mid-morning, I was delighted to see my ten-pounder, apparently none the worse for his traumatic experience of seven days before. There were two other fish with him, and neither of them had I seen before. They were too small, both being about four pounds; they certainly had not been present the previous week. As I watched the three fish drift slowly over the gravel, I noticed a large tail leisurely waving under the edge of the mid-river streamer, and presently a colossal fish emerged from the cover and slowly swam up alongside the ten-pounder. It dwarfed it. I caught my breath in excitement. I had stumbled across a barbel that looked every ounce of thirteen pounds. Minutes later, three other barbel, all over eight pounds, entered the swim, and it was becoming rapidly obvious that here I had something very special indeed. What is more, I apparently had it all to myself.

Despite intense effort, I was to catch no more barbel that season. Shortly after that very exciting sighting, the rain came and coloured the river, and a succession of chub were all that rewarded my lonely vigil. The following season was one of unbearable frustration. The poor summer meant that the Cherwell was permanently coloured, and without being able to locate the fish visually I was really up against it. They are highly localized anyway, and having to fish blind into the bargain reduced my chances drastically. All season I managed a solitary seven-pounder from the river, and that was more by luck than by judgement.

And so that brings us to July 1989. My daughter Jacqueline was on her school holidays, and I had promised her a day out fishing with me. I was at the time deeply engrossed in a Queenford bream campaign, and as that is perhaps the worst fishery to take a youngster to, since hardly anything happens at the best of times, I decided on a trip to the Cherwell. I was not going to fish specifically for barbel. A very big head of easily spotted chub would give Jacqui plenty to keep her interested.

On our arrival I was pleased to see the river low and clear, and was even more pleased to spot a barbel straight away in the same swim where I had taken the ten-pounder. It only looked about six pounds, but I fed in a load of hemp and corn, with the intention of having a crack for it later. Even an average-size barbel would be a monster to a twelve-year-old. While we were waiting for the barbel to settle on to the feed, we wandered up and down the river, and I managed to catch a couple of chub for Jacqui to look at, and she was thoroughly enjoying herself. The six-pound barbel, however, steadfastly refused to pick up a bait, and Jacqui had to be content with watching the fish in the shallow water. In mid-afternoon I found a shoal of chub under the overhanging branches of a large willow, and had them taking floating crust and corn with great confidence. Jacqui and I were standing together watching them alongside some marginal brambles when a movement caught the corner of my eye. Something had moved right at my feet, under the high bank. I stared at the downstream edge of the brambles for a minute or so, watching the water in the margins. The trailing fronds of a bed of streamer protruded from under the bramble roots, and then I spotted it, an unmistakable barbel tail. But what a tail! Straight away, I thought of the fish I had seen two years before, and watched the spot in impatient expectation. Slowly, I made out the massive form of an enormous barbel, and, just as I was trying

to direct Jacqui's eyes to the correct position, the barbel very obligingly swam slowly out from under the cover and drifted downstream. It was huge. I could not tell whether it was the same fish I had seen before, but I felt certain that it was. Again, I estimated it at as much as possibly thirteen pounds. The fish was very long indeed. In fact, if it was as fat as my ten-pounder, it might well have weighed over fourteen.

After I spotted that fish the day took on a new meaning. For several hours I patiently baited that swim with hemp and corn, resisting the temptation to fish too soon. I could not stay after dark because of Jacqui, but decided to leave it as late as possible before introducing a hookbait.

In the early evening, we crept into position, and I carefully swung out three grains of corn on a size 4 Au Lion d'Or to 8lb Maxima. The bait had hardly settled when there was a wrench on the rod, and I was soon disappointed to see a three-pound chub doing a very effective job of disturbing the swim. Still, Jacqui was pleased enough.

Ten minutes later, another carefully positioned hookbait was taken with a bang, and, when I struck, for the second time, I knew I had connected with the leviathan. It took off in a powerful run across the river, with the clutch screaming, and headed towards a tangle of fallen willow branches. I managed to stop that run, but when the barbel changed his tactics and decided to dive into the bramble roots, disaster struck. I knew that I could not allow him under there, or I would be hopelessly snagged. I clamped the clutch and hung on grimly. Right round to the handle the Tricast rod bent, as the fish battled against the intense pressure. The line made that ominous tinny creaking noise, and then, with a crack you could have heard a hundred yards away, the line parted and the barbel was gone. I sat back on my seat, the limp line fluttering in the evening breeze. I was absolutely devastated. Jacqui, showing a maturity well beyond her years, wisely said nothing for a few minutes.

What followed was quite amazing. Only about ten minutes after I had lost the fish, it once again emerged from under the near bank and swam upstream past us, only a few inches under the surface. It was almost as if it were deliberately tormenting me. This second chance to see the size of that barbel at close quarters ensured that I knew I could never rest until the folds of my landing net at last closed around it.

In the weeks that followed, I managed only another couple of trips to the river, and on the first I spent five hours in chest waders, clearing a new access point to the swim in which I had lost the fish. The brambles meant that, even if I had the barbel beaten, I would have trouble landing it over the foliage and the high bank. The lovely secluded little swim I created that day, however, has only produced chub, and barbel to just over eight pounds. I have not seen the big one there since.

On 21 September, 1989, I arrived for the first of two more days' barbel fishing. As is my normal procedure, several swims were prebaited with hemp and corn, but, unusually, after four hours I had still not seen a single barbel over the bait. Obviously, for some reason the fish preferred to stay in swims with good cover, and so one particular swim, which was in the middle of dense cabbages, drew me like a magnet. I had never before caught anything there but chub, but something told me that today would be different.

In late afternoon, I lowered a corn bait gently to rest alongside the cabbages, keeping faith with a size 4 Au Lion d'Or but having reverted to 10lb Maxima in view of the snags. The hooklink was silkworm, which I was using for the first time, and

which looked very impressive indeed. As is normal with a barbel swim which has been carefully baited over several hours without being disturbed, the bite was immediate. There were no preliminaries. One moment the rod was lying quite still in my hand, the next it was bending irresistibly towards the water. A tremendous upheaval under the cabbages preceded a very fast run downstream from a strong fish, which I knew straight away was a good barbel. For a good ten minutes it fought, twice having me snagged in the cabbages, but luckily everything held and eventually I got the upper hand. A broad flank slid over the rim of the net, and then I felt a momentary tinge of disappointment. There was that unmistakable distorted pectoral fin. The fish was undoubtedly my old friend of two years before, now two ounces lighter at 10lb 1oz.

The next day was extremely interesting in that, as well as catching two more barbel of 6lb 14oz and 8lb 5oz, I was able to observe several others apparently spooking badly at the sight of sweetcorn. This happened in two swims, and I decided that, on my next trip, I would substitute casters for the corn. Little did I imagine, when I made that decision, the size of the first fish that was to result.

A week later, I was again on the banks of the lovely River Cherwell, and had decided to bait the swim from which I had caught the ten-pounder all day, without once attempting to put a bait in until just on dusk. If there were other big fish in residence, I wanted them to have the maximum opportunity to feed in peace. During the day, the swim was fed with half a gallon of hemp and 3 pints of casters, and I whiled away the rest of the daylight hours by fishing an interesting run about thirty yards upstream. I had actually seen a shoal of bream there, including one fish that looked all of eight pounds, and felt that it would be a bit of fun trying to catch one. In that I failed; they were seemingly not interested in anything. I did, however, fluke a bonus barbel of 8lb 15oz.

The light was fading fast as I patiently baited my size 6 hook with twelve casters, and, as I carefully swung the bait into position, I was not to know that my date with destiny was only minutes away. Thirty seconds later, the line tightened and then the rod top plunged downwards. As I struck, there was an almighty swirl, and almost under my feet a great tail lashed the surface, before rocketing off upstream under some overhanging alders. I almost stopped breathing at that moment; I knew I had hooked a monster. In keeping with the size of the fish, the scrap was indeed memorable. The security of the 10lb line enabled me to apply heavy pressure from the word go, but the barbel still managed to snag me solidly in some mid-river rushes. After several minutes of pulling from all angles, I knew that there was no alternative but to go in the river. That was a slightly precarious exercise, as the high bank at that point meant that I was some four feet above the water surface and, as there is a deep hole under the bank, it would be a bit like stepping off the edge of the world. Nevertheless, I had to go in and, grabbing my landing net, I sat down on the bank and slid over the edge. I was to get a pleasant surprise. Just under the surface of the water, I found myself standing on a mud bank, and from this position I was able to play the barbel much more comfortably. That discovery was to prove invaluable in the coming weeks. With the new angle of pull my fresh position allowed, I was lucky enough to be able to free the fish from the snag, although there were still several arm-aching and very tense minutes before the net mesh at long last closed round it. As I lifted, I knew I had caught something extra-special. After I had hauled myself

and the fish up the bank and examined my prize, I saw straight away that it was the barbel I had been after. It was enormously long, but quite slender in relation to its length. Compared with the ten-pounder, it was very streamlined. Because of that, it did not weigh quite as much as I had estimated, but who was complaining when the Avons finally settled at 12lb 5oz, a new record for the Cherwell? My jubilation is hard to describe on paper; it all felt so very unreal.

Within a couple of hours, I was thinking rationally again, and, although I had taken a few self-portrait photographs, using my tripod and cable release, I knew that I had to get the fish witnessed and photographed properly. Who better to witness such a historic capture than my old mate Trefor? About an hour and a half after I telephoned him, we stood together on the banks of that delightful little river, where we have shared so many wonderful angling memories, admiring that magnificent barbel.

A little later, photographic session over, we stood in the shallows, making sure that the fish was fully recovered before releasing it. As it swam strongly away, I wondered whether I would ever make its acquaintance again, when it might indeed weigh over thirteen pounds.

Having caught such a magnificent fish, my first reaction was to move on to a different stretch of river. Surely I had exhausted the possibilities of the comparatively short length I had at my disposal. I did, however, receive information that another barbel of 10lb 10oz had been foul-hooked by a casual angler, and from the description of the fish it was certainly neither of the big fish I had taken. Apparently, this new fish was very distinctive in that it was extremely short but exceptionally deep in the flank. Obviously, in the water, this barbel might look no more than eight pounds, and I decided that, before

What dreams are made of – at 12lb 5oz this is a Cherwell record.

moving on, I would try to catch this newly discovered target.

The following Thursday saw very different weather conditions from those of the preceding weeks. The warm, dry and settled conditions had at last been broken with a vengeance, and as I baited several swims with a combination of hemp and pints of maggots, the wind was howling and rain falling steadily. It was a grey, overcast autumn scene. The rain had been with us for two days, and enough had fallen to ensure that the river was a few inches up and carrying enough colour to make observation of the fish impossible.

Because of the colour in the water, I decided to fish with luncheon meat that first night. For the first time that season, the conditions seemed ideal for a cube of 'pink inevitable', and I was full of confidence as I lowered the bait into the first swim. Seconds later, the tip pulled round, but my strike met with much feebler resistance than I anticipated, and a three-pound chub could do little about 10lb line and a size 4 hook. None the worse for his traumatic experience, he was returned about two hundred yards upstream. In the next half-hour he was followed by two companions from the second swim I fished, the best a cracking fish of 4lb 10oz, and, after putting in a lot more hemp, I moved into swim number three. But there were to be no more bites and, after many hours of effort in perfect conditions for barbel, I turned it in and retired to the van for what remained of the night. I still await my first bite on meat from the Cherwell.

The next morning saw no cessation of the rain, and I decided to fish under the umbrella during the day in one swim, with the swimfeeder, only leaving its shelter to periodically bait the three swims I had earmarked for the after-dark session. Despite the weather, it was a very pleasant and relaxed day, and at last I broke my barbel blank at lunch time, with a hard-fighting specimen of 7lb 13oz, which led me a spirited chase in and out of the rushes.

At dusk, the rain was getting heavier and, had there been anyone there to see, they would have noticed a shadowy figure, swathed head to toe in waterproofs, creep-

ing furtively behind the head-high willowherb. A size 6 Au Lion d'Or, adorned with a writhing mass of fifteen large maggots, soon lay in ambush in the gap in the cabbages at my feet – but not for long. Perhaps three minutes after the bait had been introduced I felt the merest little pluck on my finger, not enough to strike at but sufficient to alert me to the attentions of a piscine intruder. My right arm tensed to strike and, sure enough, seconds later there was an almighty wrench on the rod. As the hook went home a terrific boil under the rod top preceded the sight of a huge barbel rolling on the surface, before it righted itself and powered away through the cabbages. Despite the rain, the night

Another perfect Cherwell double – 11lb 4oz.

was not particularly dark, and I had a very good view of a fish which I could see was very long indeed. I knew it was not the new double that I had come to catch, and throughout the fight I was convinced that I had hooked the twelve-pounder again. What a truly memorable scrap that barbel gave me! For fully fifteen minutes the battle ebbed and flowed, and when I eventually netted the fish, again having had to slide into the river to accomplish that man-oeuvre, my right arm was nearly numb from the muscle-aching encounter.

Laying fish and net carefully on the soft wet grass, I fumbled in my bag for the torch to examine my prize. The first thing I looked at was the tail, and for that very distinctive scar the twelve-pounder bore. But there was none. It was a different fish after all – but which one? It certainly was not my ten-pounder, and no way did it fit the description of the foul-hooked barbel. I could feel the excitement mounting within me as I zeroed the Avons, and when the needle finally steadied it took me some time to realize the significance of what I saw before me. Eleven pounds four ounces was the weight I recorded, from a barbel that had never been caught before, and certainly had until then avoided showing itself, despite my years of fishing the river, most of that time in the clear conditions of summer.

With the barbel safely reposing in a ca-pacious carp sack, I poured a cup of tea and tried to take it all in. That one fish had changed everything. If one double-figure barbel could hide itself from me for so long, so could others. Far from moving on, the stretch warranted even closer atten-tion. When I eventually drove home that night, I reflected on the fact that I had taken three doubles in consecutive weeks, all different fish and from a river where the capture of any barbel is a fairly rare event, let alone a double-figure fish. Two of these

fish had beaten the previous river record, and I had certainly created my own little piece of angling history.

The following Thursday I was to make the score four doubles in four weeks, and this capture showed the importance of being able to recognize individual fish in accurately assessing the potential of a stretch of river (considered at length in Chapter 10). When I landed a barbel after dark, which turned the scales at 10lb 12oz, at first I thought I had located yet another different specimen. Closer examination, however, revealed several tell-tale identi-fication marks. The fish was undoubtedly my eleven-pounder of six days before, now eight ounces lighter, and completed a ter-rific brace of fish, as I had taken a 9lb 1oz specimen earlier.

Recapture of the 11lb 4oz fish – now weighing 10lb 12oz.

Top class Oxford angler, Simon Lush, with a huge Cherwell barbel at 12lb 1½oz.

My luck was to run out the following week. I was prematurely congratulating myself on making it five out of five, as I played a monstrous fish in the darkness. For several minutes I was in total control of the proceedings, and the fish had rolled several times, showing me that it was a good double. With one last effort, it shot across river, making the clutch scream, and then there was an ominous lack of movement. The fish had found an unsuspected snag, and nothing I tried could shift it. It ended with me in the river, well over the top of both waders, but there was to be no happy ending. After a good half-hour of stalemate, there was a sudden surge from the fish and the line, obviously weakened by the constant abrasion, parted with a sickening crack. It was a sad angler who squelched his way back to the van that night.

A catch of fish the following week persuaded me to give the barbel a rest for a while, as the five I took included three recognizable fish of 7lb 14oz, 8lb 8oz and 9lb 11oz, which had all lost quite a bit of weight. The nine-pounder was my old favourite, which I had taken earlier in the season at 10lb 1oz, and so showed a weight loss of 6oz.

The other two fish had shown similar losses and I reasoned that they were perhaps suffering from the stress of being pursued so intently. I would leave them alone for a while to recover and, I hoped, regain the lost ounces. Those magnificent fighters deserved a break. But I would be back. They could be assured of that.

7 A Royalty Dream

Trefor West

Back in the late sixties, in the winter of 1968 to be precise, I discovered the famous Royalty fisheries at Christchurch in Hampshire. It was about that time that embryo specialist angler West began to venture far and wide in search of specimen fish. Of course, I had read of the Dorset Stour Throop fisheries and The Royalty on the Avon, and the specimens of every species they contained, and for months after my first tentative steps into the hallowed ground of Christchurch the only thought

The Housepool on the Royalty.

91

that preceded sleep was that of a grinning Westy holding a record roach, barbel or chub.

Little did I know that that first weekend was the start of a love affair that is as strong today as it was all those years ago. Christchurch is still a place where I feel at ease, the Stour and Avon still Mecca for barbel anglers. I have flirted with the Wensum for a few seasons, and I am in the middle of an affair with the Bristol Avon at the moment. Despite those interludes elsewhere, the Stour and Hampshire Avon will always hold that special place in my affections.

The Royalty has an undeserved 'easy' tag, a legacy of the maggot saturation days of the early seventies, when catches of a dozen fish from the Pipe slack, with three doubles, was not unusual. The Railway Pool, home of the reputed monsters of the Avon, turned up ten- and eleven-pound fish daily. Six-pound chub hardly rated a mention in the angling press, unless, of course, you caught a brace of them. Heady days indeed, and ones that are long gone and not likely to return.

Today's Royalty scene is a totally different proposition. The number of doubles the fishery contains would probably not amount to any more than the catch return from any one week in the heyday of yesteryear. However, it is not just about extra-big fish, but enjoyment, involvement with the fishing and those special methods now needed to extract a Royalty barbel. The place has a feel, a true tradition. Just think of the famous anglers who have stood in the swims we fish today, men such as Wallis, Walker, Harrigan and, perhaps most successful of them all, the legendary Bill Warren. It's nice to think that they may all be somewhere having a drink together, and recounting tales of monsters hooked, lost or landed. If I had a pound for every hour I have spent on the banks of the Royalty, I could retire tomorrow and spend the rest of my days fishing. With that delightful thought, let us go back to that special day in this special place, when I at last made contact with a very special fish – a Royalty double.

The grey December day had taken its toll of anglers and, save for one individual huddled behind his umbrella in the Railway Pool, the banks were deserted. The river was carrying the remnants of the heavy rain of the previous day, and the water temperature of 44°F (7°C) was sufficient to keep the barbel in feeding mood and provide bites throughout the day. Barbel of 6lb 10oz, 7lb 6oz and 4lb had been landed, which, together with two other missed chances, ensured that I was deeply absorbed in the fishing and the technique needed to fool one of the canny Royalty barbel into intercepting my luncheon-meat hookbait.

A fast pick-up, and an equally fast rejection, brought a smile to my face. In the blink of an eye another chance had been missed. I swore to myself, but realized that the barbel responsible had probably been an old friend, and knew what to expect. He would not be tempted again, so I moved on towards the bottom of the Trammels, my favourite swim on the whole of the Royalty fishery. I have caught dozens of eight- and nine-pound fish from that short thirty-yard stretch of river, its smooth surface concealing weedbeds and gravel depressions, the near bank turbulence resulting from a large bed of ranunculus and bank erosion caused by countless years of coping with the Avon's heavy winter flows.

The water surface is smooth from ten feet out to the far-bank rushes, an area beloved by chub. Indeed, as I gazed across the water my memory recalled three scale-perfect chub I had taken one day – fish of 4lb 4oz, 4lb 8oz and 4lb 14oz – by casting crust upstream and across into the mouth of the little weir. What price can you put on your angling memories?

The swim looked good, and I was sure that its consistency in producing a bite would continue. More than once it had provided a face-saving bite on a day when all seemed lost, and I had a feeling that once again it would not let me down. As the light faded in the evening of that overcast December day, an inch cube of meat plopped into the flow upstream and across from my position, opposite the mouth of the sidestream from the little weir. As the half-ounce lead hit bottom, the pick-up of my Abu Cardinal 54 was engaged as the Avon's flow picked up the slack line. Seconds later, I could feel the lead tripping over the gravel, the fingers of my left hand holding the line under light tension, ensuring that no movement of the terminal rig would go unnoticed.

The lead's progress was halted by the remnants of the mid-river weedbed. A biteless couple of minutes later, a lift of the rod and a tweak of the line in my left hand successfully dislodged the lead and started it on its way again downstream. Each bump and bounce could be observed on the quivertip and felt on my fingers. Again the lead stopped, caught up on another weed root, the exact spot where a 9¼-pounder had accepted a similarly presented bait only a few weeks before, as had many other barbel I had landed from the swim over the years. Today, however, there was no response. I moved the lead

An old friend – weighing in at 10lb 4oz.

again, and it began to swing across the flow. At this, I lost interest in the cast, as the correct presentation and control were gone, and retrieved the tackle.

Fumbling around in my Barbour coat pocket, I eventually located a ¾oz lead and in seconds it was on the snap link swivel. Impaling a fresh cube of meat, I once more cast just past mid-river. The lead settled, moved once, and then held in position. It was my intention this time to present a much more slowly moving bait, leaving it stationary for at least half a minute between movements of the lead. The bait had moved six or seven times, and was now in mid-river, when I detected a pluck and slight release of tension on my finger, followed immediately by a slow draw on the line. The classic barbel bite!

The strike pulled the hook home and for a while the barbel hung there in mid-river, before backing off, curving the rod into an exciting arc. I knew it was a good fish, and as I leaned into it to make it move the barbel shook its head and kited towards the far bank. Slowly, it began to plod upstream, every yard being accompanied by great thumps on the rod top. At that moment I felt sure that this was the Avon double I felt I deserved. Soon the barbel was level with my position, and I piled on pressure in an attempt to lift it off the bottom and pull the fish towards me into the main near-bank flow. I knew that if I could achieve that the fish would turn and run downstream, which was exactly what I wanted the big barbel to do. However, she stubbornly refused to be moved in my direction, and thumped the rod top even more savagely in disdain at my efforts to dictate proceedings. Not an inch of line had been lost or gained as the rod top absorbed each swaying movement of the fish, and for a time it was stalemate. I bent the rod a little more, way past the curvature recommended by the manufacturers. I sensed the barbel

gradually yielding a yard at a time, and I kept her moving into the fast flow. Once in the main push of water, I felt her suddenly turn downstream, and the rod wrenched round as she belted off down river, the clutch screaming its music in my ears. Twenty yards of line ripped from the reel in seconds. I remember saying out loud: 'That's why I fish for these things, because they can do that.'

I followed her downstream, retrieving the line I had lost, and then piled on the pressure once again. Slowly, the barbel moved back upstream, against the flow. She was not so deep down in the water now, and provided I did not make any silly mistakes, and good luck was on my side, the fish was mine. A further ten yards upstream she moved, with me following about two yards behind, until we were back in our original position. Another fifteen-yard run downstream was much slower and, as I again followed, the line was easily retrieved as I felt the fight ebbing from that mighty barbel. Tired as she was, though, she still possessed that adrenalin-pumping power that I love so much.

Shortly afterwards I had her on a tight line under the rod point, and once more she attempted to move upstream. This time, however, she lacked the strength to fight both the current and the twelve feet of carbon that was restraining her. Gently, I eased the barbel up in the water, a foot at a time, letting her go down again whenever she made a last despairing effort. Eventually I caught a glimpse of silver belly, and then she at last broke surface and I could see her clearly. I knew that it was a double-figure barbel for sure at that moment. Gently, the fish was led downstream, into the near-bank slack eddy where the bank had been eroded away, and then that magnificent barbel was slowly pulled over the rim of the landing net. The fish went in with just the merest flick of that great tail,

The Railway Pool – home of legendary monsters.

and then I lifted my prize from the water. I carried her well away from the water's edge, laid the fish on some soft grass, pulled away the mesh and removed the hook. That manoeuvre complete, I sat back and looked in admiration at the superbly conditioned barbel before me. I can recall actually talking to the fish. 'Well, girl,' I said, 'you took a long time coming, didn't you? And didn't you put up one hell of a scrap for your freedom?' The barbel's mouth moved at that moment, almost as though she were agreeing with me. 'You are a beauty,' I said, 'and very well worth waiting for.' At that, I slipped the fish into the weigh-bag, lifted it onto the scales, and

watched as they confirmed what I already knew. The barbel was indeed a double 10lb 10oz of sheer perfection.

For fifteen minutes I held that barbel in the flow to recover her strength fully, after which she clamped her huge pectorals into the gravel to hold station unaided. I smoked two cigarettes as she lay there. It was by now fully dark, and she seemed to be bigger than ever in the torchlight, almost larger than life. Then, with a flick of her tail, she was gone.

I have had larger barbel, both before and since, but that first Royalty double is, and always will be, a very special fish. It was the fulfilment of a Royalty dream.

8   Floodwater Fishing

Over the years, some of our most memorable catches of barbel have been taken during winter floods, reinforcing the fact that, provided the temperature is favourable, such conditions promote uninhibited feeding. As we said in Chapter 5, it is important to take into account the conditions that preceded the flood. We would not expect the same level of success if the flood had been caused by melting snow, as opposed to warm rain, for instance. Almost always, however, extra water means that we are in business.

The first thing to understand about fishing a winter flood is that it is still vital to look for areas where current speed and surface characteristics are right. Although well adapted to hold position in the strongest

Returning an eleven-pounder to a flooded great Ouse.

A cracking Bristol Avon barbel of 12lb 10oz.

Trefor with a hard fighting eleven-pounder.

13lb 2oz of solid muscle.

Back she goes.

A winter barbel river in perfect trim.

Matthew Bodily with a magnificently conditioned Ouse fish.

Tony's 14lb 2oz fish, which has since been caught at over 16lb.

Streamer weed and barbel go together.

Our old mate Merv Wilkinson with a superb Warks Avon specimen.

Heavily spiced meat tempted this gorgeous fish from the Ouse.

Tony's last big Cherwell barbel – 11lb 7oz to a bunch of maggots.

Top barbel angler Adrian Busby with a clonking thirteen-pounder.

Tony's personal best, a fabulous 14lb 7oz Ouse monster.

A brilliant Ouse brace.

Another leviathan from the Great Ouse, 13lb 8oz.

Red corn/red maggot, an irresistible cocktail.

Colour coded designer barbel pastes.

The condom rig.

Maggots superglued to a polyball creates the Medusa rig.

Stuart Morgan cradles a lovely twelve-pounder.

The most high profile stretch of the Ouse, home to monstrous barbel.

A Hants Avon weir at sunset.

Upstream meat proved the downfall of this lovely barbel.

Trefor rests a big barbel in the net before returning it.

flows, barbel will still seek out a speed of flow as similar as possible to that to which they are generally accustomed. The depth is totally irrelevant, and some of the old advice about looking for a deep hole or eddy in a flood we believe to be immensely misleading. With heavy colour in the water, the barbel will feed happily in swims less than 18 inches deep. Eddies in particular we have absolutely no time for, especially in flood conditions. In high water, they are frequently turbulent, with the result that flotsam is continually swirled around by the ever-varying currents – exactly the environment that any self-respecting barbel is going to avoid like the plague. We are looking for evenly paced flows – up to a fast walking pace is ideal, with that all-important smooth surface.

It is also of little importance how short the swim is, as one only a few feet long can harbour a group of big fish. Many good floodwater swims will be found in the shelter of the banks and in the lee of obstacles of one kind or another, and some of these areas can be very short indeed. As well as having a nice even pace, it is vital that the water surface is as smooth as possible, indicating fairly even bottom contours. Constant surface turbulence will continually lift bottom debris and, although the occasional small vortex does no harm, a swim which is continually boiling is useless, and does not even warrant a cast.

At this point, it is interesting to consider one type of winter swim that goes from good to poor and then to good again as the water level rises, and that is the area which is usually a shallow run containing a bed of streamer weed. In normal winter conditions it may be about eighteen inches deep, and of fairly smooth surface, and would be a reasonable bite producer in favourable temperatures. With one or two feet of extra water in the river, the weedbed begins to

undulate rapidly, creating boils and substantial turbulence, and the swim now becomes one which the barbel will soon vacate. However, with another two feet of floodwater, the depth approaches six feet, and this can actually result in the surface smoothing out again, as the additional volume of water cancels out the undulating effect of the weed. Far from being the poor swim it was, it now reverts to being an excellent one. A fast shallow has in effect been transformed into a smooth, steady glide which, although still fast, is at least uniform.

Flood conditions create many new areas of interest. As we are looking for a smooth, steady glide of whatever depth, the first area that comes to mind is the flooded cattle drink, which may normally be only inches deep over fine gravel. Many rivers take the form of wide, shallow areas connected by narrower, faster channels, and when the river is high in flood the margins of these pools can be several feet deep, steadily moving, and a natural harbour, where the barbel can escape the uncomfortable turbulence of other areas.

Fascinating floodwater fishing can be experienced in the small swims created when bankside bushes become partially submerged. As the water rises, the foliage of each bush acts like a brake to the current, and creates a small lee of steadier water behind itself. It may even temporarily divert the main flow a little towards midstream, causing a very seductive little crease. Such swims act as a magnet for winter barbel, as they do for many other species. The upstream legering technique we described earlier is deadly for fishing swims of this type, from the opposite bank. A line of bushes can be effectively searched very efficiently, and a great many barbel have succumbed in this manner.

When upstreaming across a fast current, however, be aware that the increased flow

The School Bridge at Throop – submerged.

may mean that the normal slack-line bite may not occur, or if it does it happens too quickly to detect. What happens is that, immediately a barbel picks up the bait and disturbs the balance, creating slack, the fast flow immediately picks up the line and keeps it under tension. The usual bite is therefore more likely to be a complete movement of the lead under tension than the true slack-line indication you would experience in the gentler flows of normal winter level.

As well as partially submerged bankside foliage, the lee of quiet water behind mid-river obstacles creates superb flood swims. In fact, the faster the river becomes the better some of these swims can get, as the difference in current speed becomes more marked. Obviously, at some stage, the onset of turbulence will determine when you have too much of a good thing.

At times like this, the benefit of knowing your river becomes apparent. Mid-river rush beds provide superb swims downstream of themselves when they die off in the winter. During very high water the remains of the rushes will obviously be hidden, but, knowing their location, you can

fish baits behind the shelter they afford. Once again, upstream legering is by far the best presentation.

Obviously, holding a bait in a steadier flow in mid-river, when the intervening current may be racing through, will require a great deal more lead than if you were fishing a near-bank run. But it must hold position, and you must not be afraid to put enough lead on to achieve that objective. If a swim requires 2oz for the correct presentation, then use 2oz. You will still be fishing sensitively, since almost all of the mass of the terminal rig will be counterbalanced by the speed of the flow and the drag on the line. Only a small additional pull will therefore be required to disturb that balance and move the bait, and the chances are that that is a bite.

Very recently the Kennet was in full flood, bursting its banks in many places. A long, straight section appeared very daunting, full of turbulent, angry-looking boils, caused by submerged bushes, trees and clay boulders where the bank had collapsed. From a long way upstream, a small flat spot in midstream stuck out like a sore thumb to the experienced eye. The problem was how to hold the lead and bait static in that smooth flow, amongst the turbulent, powerful currents that surrounded it. Upstreaming was impractical because of bankside vegetation. The lead was changed from 1½oz to 2½oz, and a forty-yard cast was made across and downstream, the terminal rig landing in the faster water across and upstream of the flat spot. The lead hit bottom and immediately began to pull across into midstream, whereupon the rod top was pointed directly in line with the bait. The lead continued to swing across the flow, out of the far bank turbulence, in a series of bounces, until it finally held in the smooth water. As a finger was curled round the line, with the rod still pointing at the bait, the tremendous pressure could easily be felt as the flow attempted to dislodge the lead. The whole set-up was as taut as a banjo string, but balanced for all that. A bite from a barbel could have taken the form of a simple sudden movement of lead, a firm downstream pull, or a momentary release of tension followed by a heavier tension than was felt previously. In fact, the third version occurred, resulting in a superb winter fish of 7lb 12oz, which was just one of no fewer than twenty-seven barbel caught in two days in a bank-high February Kennet flood. The moral is not to worry about the amount of lead you have to use. Keep piling it on until you can present a bait correctly in areas that appear suitable. If you need more lead to hold, then do not be afraid to use it.

In murky flood conditions barbel feed entirely by smell, and baits such as meat and cheese are a must. They should always be fished static. You rarely experience bites when the lead and bait are moving, but as soon as they stop a bite can occur at any time. So good are flood conditions, when the temperature is favourable, that a bite may be expected within seconds of the bait coming to rest, and it stands to reason that the more potential holding spots your bait is introduced to the greater your chances of locating and therefore catching barbel. Three two-minute casts are better than one six-minute cast. If nothing is happening in a good-looking swim, the barbel are not there, and you will be well advised to move to a different swim. You can always return later, when barbel may well have moved in. We know, from our extensive experience with winter barbel under these conditions, that if a bait settles within a barbel's smell range the fish will be onto it in seconds, and therefore half an hour in a swim is likely to include twenty-five wasted minutes. It is far more productive to move, move and move again.

Having had a bite and taken a barbel from a swim, the chances are that there may be other fish to be caught in the same area. However, if there is no immediate response, do not flog away, spooking the fish even more than they might be. It is better to rest the swim, let the barbel recover from their alarm, and return later, when another immediate bite should be the reward for your patience.

One of the major problems with fishing in floodwater is the one of surface and subsurface rubbish collecting on the line. Although it is always annoying, you can actually use it to your advantage by again fishing upstream, providing of course that ridiculous amounts of debris are not being carried down. In an upstreaming situation, a slow build-up of rubbish on the line can actually do the job of periodically moving the bait for you. As the water pressure on the rubbish gets too great for the lead, it will shift its position, and a great deal of the flotsam becomes dislodged and floats away, allowing the lead to resettle. When fishing in this manner, which is making the best of a bad job, it pays to strike at all unusual movements, though many will be found to be caused by rubbish. The correct mental attitude is required: you must be prepared to accept that many false strikes are going to be made. But it is preferable to strike at false bites than not to strike at indications that were caused by barbel. With experience, you can tell which of the many indications are true bites, and each success instils more confidence. A classic example of the above from Tony's diaries is a never-to-be-forgotten weekend trip to Throop. Many days of torrential rain had ensured that so bad was the flooding that at least one entire garden shed came floating past. The amounts of rubbish were such that the tackle had to be cleared every few minutes, but mixed in with all the false bites were five real ones, yielding four seven-pound barbel and

A chunky seven-pounder is slipped back into a flooded Bristol Avon.

a top fish of 8lb 2oz. A good maxim is, if in doubt, strike. You will do far less damage to a swim by striking at possible false bites that you would in lower, clear conditions. To have struck and missed is better than no strike at all.

The barbel are actively on the prowl for food in floodwater conditions, knowing as they do the volume of natural fodder that is washed downstream by the heavy currents. All kinds of aquatic life, such as shrimps and caddis, which may be normally hard to find, are disturbed and become easy prey for once. The barbel's streamlined shape is well adapted to take advantage of so much good grub on the hoof, and they will be right there in the flow, feeding furiously. Although they will be in the steady, smooth flows, they will not be skulking in slacks,

waiting for the flood to subside. A flood is a time of plenty for the barbel, and a time of equal plenty for us barbel catchers, if we learn how to cope with the conditions.

Among the most reliable of floodwater swims is the high, vertical bank, especially if somewhere along its length is an under-cut or two. Close to the near bank on the bottom the flow can be very steady, even though the surface may initially appear far too fast for comfortable fishing. The reason for this is that vertical banks alongside a reasonable depth of water exert a tremen-dous drag on the flow, and this is most marked at the riverbed. A stretch of deep water between high banks will always have its fastest current at the surface in mid-river, assuming that there are no obstacles to the current's path.

The differences in flow rate between the surface and bottom water alongside the near bank can be demonstrated quite simply. Using a quivertip, set up initially with a link weight much lighter than you think would be required for the speed of the flow that you can actually see on the surface, and then lower the terminal rig a few feet away from the bank. Initially, the tackle will be very taut and the tip bent right round, as the light rig is washed round by the fast current, until eventually it rests on the bottom, hard against the near bank, When the rig comes to rest, the tip will ease back, and you will be able to fish normally. The light terminal rig has

8lb 2oz – a floodwater reward from Throop.

automatically searched out the steadiest flow. This is an absolutely deadly presentation for winter barbel, and many of the very big Dorset Stour and Hampshire Avon fish are caught in exactly this way every year.

We started this chapter with a passing reference to the superb catches of barbel that have been taken from floodwater. Let us end it with a quick look at some outstanding examples. There was the catch of thirteen fish to 9lb 14oz from the Railway Pool on the Royalty, when water was spilling into the fields, and the eighteen fish to 7¼lb from Ironbridge on the Severn, when the river was carrying seven feet of turbid brown floodwater. Trefor can recall fish of 8lb 6oz, 8lb 12oz and 8lb 14oz in three casts on the Wensum, when he had to stand in a foot of water in the field to fish; and a flooded Cherwell provided six fish in rapid succession to Tony one night, a catch that included fish of 9lb 6oz and 9lb 9oz. There have been several catches of ten and a dozen fish from the Bristol Avon, when more than two feet of extra water has been raging down the Avon valley, and on one breathtaking night there fish of 8lb 6oz, 8lb 8oz, 8lb 12oz, 9lb 1oz, 9lb 7oz and 10lb 2oz found meat baits irresistible. Is it any wonder that we consider perfect conditions to be a river at least two feet above normal winter level, carrying plenty of colour, with a water temperature of 46°F (8°C) and steady continuous rain to keep the level stable? Those are the kind of conditions when the average angler either stays at home or is tucked up beneath an umbrella. For the serious barbel angler, they spell paradise.

Floodwater conditions are the most productive of all for barbel catching. They may look daunting at first, but, with a little experience, they present no greater problem than any other conditions. The barbel are out there, actively searching for food. Basic legering techniques, plus both additional lead and a pound or two of determination, will see you well on your way to experiencing the most exciting and productive barbel fishing of your life. So, when your river comes into flood, be there!

9   A Stour Double

Tony Miles

Of all specimen fish, the target that took me the longest to achieve was a barbel of over ten pounds in weight. By the end of the season in March 1986, after another hard winter on the Wensum which had still seen my ambition unfulfilled, I vowed that I would not rest until I had cracked that magical barrier. After all, my personal best fish of 9lb 12oz had been taken no less than fourteen years earlier, and I was certainly due a change of fortune where an extra-big barbel was concerned.

During the close season I spoke at length to Stef Horak, who I had recently met at TC pit, and who knew the southern rivers, and in particular the Dorset Stour, like the back of his hand. Although a Midlander, Stef had lived for some considerable time in Dorset and had an enviable record with the big barbel of that part of the world. During our many conversations Stef put me on the right track in terms of stretches of the Stour that had produced double-figure fish, and I would like to record here my thanks to him for the invaluable information he gave me at the time.

Stef's enthusiasm for the Stour was infectious and fired in me the ambition to spend a season on the river in the renewed search for that ten-pound-plus specimen. I was in need of a change. Although Trefor had taken many double-figure fish from the Wensum, it was not being at all kind to me, and my barbel fishing was becoming a little stale as a consequence.

My first session, on a stretch of river I had never before seen let alone fished, was made in August. I was there for two days and spent the bulk of the first just looking around, noting where all the various features were, and putting bait in plenty of swims. It was an ideal day for a first acquaintance, being bright and sunny, and this, coupled with the low, clear water, made observation very easy. I saw barbel everywhere I looked, and it was obvious that there was a substantial head of them present. The average fish seemed to be about seven pounds or so, but in two areas I saw fish that looked as though they were much bigger. As I stood on the high bank overlooking one particularly inviting-looking swim alongside rushes, three or four big fish drifted into view over the clear gravel. I put them all at over nine pounds, but one individual looked every ounce of eleven. I had found what I was looking for.

Over the next few hours I concentrated my baiting programme on just four swims, where at least one big fish had been in evidence, and soon had fish feeding avidly in two of them. I was very excited to observe the eleven-pounder with its snout buried in the hemp, and was confident that success was assured.

Because of the conditions, daytime fishing was obviously going to revolve round the use of particle baits, and so I had introduced a quantity of casters and maggots in conjunction with the hemp. My first cast,

A STOUR DOUBLE

A remote stretch of the Stour.

104

with a swimfeeder rig baited with three casters, proved the error of this tactic. Within seconds I had a good pull and soon landed a horrible little bootlace eel, and when this was followed by another, and then another, it was time for a rethink. I lowered two more droppers of hemp into the swim, this time each one containing a dozen grains of corn, and then rested the swim. Mistakenly, I thought that the eels would leave the corn alone. I was wrong. They seemed to love it as much as they did the casters and maggots.

As dusk approached, the eels had totally defeated my efforts to catch barbel, though one 4½lb chub had lifted the gloom a little, and I was becoming more and more agitated. I could still clearly see double-figure fish scoffing the hemp, and it was enough to make me scream in frustration. The failing light did see a barbel at last fall to a piece of meat, a fat eight-pounder, which was at least some consolation for the carpet of eels I had been forced to wade through. The second day was even more irritating. There were a lot more barbel in evidence over my hemp and corn (I had introduced no more maggots after the previous days events), but it made no difference whatever. Whichever hookbait I used on that second day, the result was the same – another damnable eel. No chub or last-minute barbel came along either, and I drove home that evening in a sullen mood, my head full of possible ways of beating those little reptilian monstrosities.

For what remained of August, and throughout September and early October, I fished the Stour every week, frequently making the long journey from Coventry just for one day's fishing. Never did I see as many fish grouped together as I did on the first trip, but most days saw a couple of fish landed. There were, however, no big ones among them, and by mid-October that initial eight-pounder still headed the list.

The autumn of that year was characterized by some very early frosts, and after one totally blank two-day session in October, when the temperature had fallen well below zero at night, I decided to call a temporary halt to my campaign. The river was still painfully low and clear and night frosts were obviously going to be the kiss of death. Conditions for barbel fishing were unlikely to improve until we had some prolonged warm rain to freshen and colour the river. When that happened, I would return.

That was the plan, anyway. A telephone call I shall never forget occurred about two hours after I had returned home from the trip. It was Stef, inquiring whether I fancied a trip to the Stour the following week, barbel fishing, as he had booked two days' holiday. Despite the conditions, he was keen to have a crack at those barbel, and so I agreed to go with him. My planned first piking trip would be postponed for a week, and in the early hours of the following Thursday I picked Stef up from home and we started the drive to Dorset.

We were on the bank at dawn and, if anything, the river looked in a sorrier state than when I had left it six days before. With frost underfoot, freezing mist in the air and a low, clear and very stale river, conditions were hardly ideal for barbel to feed well. Our fishing soon confirmed our worst fears. Bites were at a premium and I had but the one, in mid-afternoon. That came from a medium-sized barbel, which I managed to lose when it charged through some streamer. Stef was top rod with a small chub and a four-pound barbel, and not long after dark we were drowning our sorrows in a local hostelry.

As all anglers will, we talked for many hours about all aspects of catching big fish, during which the beer flowed a little too freely, and when we eventually settled down in the dubious comfort of my car I was feeling decidedly queasy. Despite the fact that the car seemed to be spinning on the spot, I managed to get to sleep, and so I remained until about two in the morning. I remember waking with a start, with the most crippling pains in my stomach and my head pounding. It was agony to move, but I somehow managed to roll out of the car, where I was instantaneously violently sick under the hedge. For over half an hour I remained crouching under those bushes on that freezing cold night, and I was convinced that I would never see the morning. I really thought that I was dying.

When I eventually crawled back into the car the sickness had passed but I had probably the worst headache I have ever experienced, and the most overwhelming feeling of nausea. All thoughts about fishing had long since disappeared. All I was interested in was going home.

I felt no better the next morning, and Stef, to his credit, offered to drive me back to Coventry, despite the fact that he had booked a holiday specially for the trip. It was attractive, but I felt very guilty at spoiling his plans. In the end I made the decision that was to prove crucial. We would drive back to the river and give it a shot. Perhaps the icy-cold early-morning air would do me some good.

After a cup of tea, some headache tablets, and a long walk to the swims over the frost-encrusted grass, my head had cleared a lot and I even started to feel some enthusiasm for fishing again. There seemed less prospect of a barbel than ever.

Tony and Martin James on the banks of the famous Throop fishery.

The night had certainly been the coldest so far, and great clouds of clammy mist hung over the water as I lowered five droppers of hemp and one of casters into my chosen swim. I had no intention of dashing about today. Sitting quietly, with a flask of tea to hand, was about as energetic as I wanted to get. Also, it would probably be the best approach in the circumstances. The barbel would certainly not tolerate being chased in the conditions we faced, and a static bait of two casters was as good a bet as any.

I had just finished the baiting when Stef joined me for a brief chat. As we stood there talking, I suddenly caught the flash of coral-pink fins deep down in the swim. Just above the bed of streamer that marked the downstream boundary of the patch of gravel on which I had deposited my hemp, the water was about five feet deep and observation was quite difficult. However, we stared intently at the spot together and, having caught the flash of large pectoral fins again, slowly started to make out the vague outline of a big barbel.

'That is a definite double', said Stef, 'You're going to be in business.' Frost or no frost, here was one fish that certainly appeared to be feeding, and at last the urge to fish was returning.

Very carefully, I lowered my bait of two casters on a size 12 hook, fished in conjunction with a small feeder loaded with hemp, to rest just above the root of that streamer bed. The steady current would ensure that the grains of hemp slowly filtered out through the enlarged holes of the feeder, and I sat there in silent anticipation.

After an hour, the morning had become quite pleasantly sunny, though still cold, and my attention had been distracted by the antics of a pair of kingfishers on the low branches of a small willow opposite. As I watched one dive the line tightened over my right forefinger, and then the rod plunged alarmingly towards the water's surface. That first run was tremendously powerful and, with the clutch whining, ten yards of line was lost in seconds. After that initial surge everything became ominously solid, and nothing I could do would shift the fish. Despite the ten yards of line I had first lost, I could see my swimfeeder lodged in the root of the streamer bed, and it was obvious that the barbel had torn through the weedbed, forcing the feeder up the line in the process.

For a good fifteen minutes I moved upstream and down, pulling as hard as I dare from every conceivable angle, but to no avail. All was totally immovable, and I reluctantly decided that I would have to pull for a break. I was by now convinced that the fish had gone and I was simply stuck in a snag. Pointing the rod down the line, I began pulling. The line tightened and then there was a sudden frantic pull. Hurriedly, I got the rod point up once more, as a further three yards was taken against the clutch. With this confirmation that the fish was still attached, I was in a quandary. I could still see the feeder, and obviously I would have no chance of ever landing the barbel if the line could not be freed from that root of streamer weed. I came to the inescapable conclusion that either I or Stef would have to go in and free it. As I pointed out to Stef, I had the important job of holding the rod. To him then would go the honour of freeing the line. Thanking me profusely for my consideration, and obviously relishing the thought of his imminent immersion into five feet of icy cold water, Stef stripped to his underpants and gingerly waded out. The chattering of Stef's teeth rose in a crescendo as he sank deeper and deeper, and then he suddenly disappeared. Obviously, he had just discovered an interesting depression.

At least he could now get no wetter, and so he could better concentrate on the job in hand. Soon he was upstream of the clump of streamer and, feeling round with his feet, he located the line. As he started to lift it, there was another savage wrench on the rod and a few more yards of line was lost. By now we had no idea of how far away the fish was, or even in which direction it had travelled. After the short run had stopped, Stef at last successfully brought the entire root of streamer to the surface, when he could see that my line almost entirely encircled it. It then became obvious what had happened. After picking up my bait the barbel had shot upstream, and not down as I had thought.

Agonisingly slowly, Stef cleared the line from the fronds, while I held the rod as high as possible, taking in the slack as it was created to avoid further snagging. Suddenly the line came free and, at that

An ambition achieved.

instant, the barbel rocketed upstream faster than ever. It must have felt the relaxation of tension in the tackle. That was quite a dangerous moment for Stef, as he was holding the line over his shoulder as it came free. When the fish shot upstream the line tightened round Stef's throat, almost garrotting him. He was forced to duck under the water again to get out of the way.

At long last I was in direct contact with the fish, but the drama was by no means over. The barbel had enjoyed a protracted rest period and was now as fresh as when I had first hooked him. Consequently, it gave me a stirring scrap for quite some considerable time before I at long last caught a sight of my adversary. When I did so, my first reaction was one of bitter disappointment, not because of the size of the fish, which was obviously big, but because it appeared to be foul-hooked. It was coming in sideways. Luckily, my worries were groundless. The line had merely taken a temporary hold round one of the large pectorals and the fish was, after all, fairly hooked.

At five yards out, the barbel kept circling a few feet down, stubbornly refusing to come any closer and with me afraid to pile on too much pressure because of the size 12 hook, which had already undergone a severe testing. It was all I could do to resist the temptation to bully the fish. Eventually my patience was rewarded, and a magnificent barbel rolled into the net. Not only was that fish memorable for being my first ever double-figure barbel, but it is the longest fight of my angling career. The fish was landed exactly one hour after it was first hooked.

I let Stef do the honours for me with the scales, and he soon announced 10lb 9oz. After nearly twenty years of fishing for big barbel, I had done it at last. Stef, who really must have been freezing cold standing there in just his wet underwear, appeared as pleased as I was. He was grinning from ear to ear as we took the photographs, and I realised at that moment that I am indeed lucky to have so many good angling friends. We also took some video film, and I remember with amusement Stef doing a dummy run with the camera, while I stood in front of him holding my arms out as though supporting an imaginary fish. That was to allow him to get used to the controls, but had people been passing at that moment, and seen a man throwing his arms around for no particular reason being filmed by another man dressed in just his underpants, God knows what they would have made of it!

10 The Importance of Recognizing Individual Fish

If, like us, you enjoy continual new challenges in your barbel fishing, both to increase the weight of personal best fish and to investigate new venues, then it is vitally important to have some means of assessing the potential of the river lengths you are fishing. In this regard, being able to recognize individual fish is crucial if you are going to be able to establish the true barbel population. The frequency of barbel recaptures – and we are talking of all fish and not just the large ones – enables us to make logical decisions based on fact and not conjecture. It also saves much potentially valuable fishing time. If you know that almost every fish is a recapture, then you can safely make the decision to move on much earlier than if you are fishing blind.

For example, a stretch of the Bristol Avon on which Trefor and Mick Nicholls have been concentrating always produces a few bites in reasonable conditions, and has always been looked upon as a banker for a barbel or two. From November until Christmas, six fish over eight pounds, including a nine-pounder, suggested a good head of large fish. Surely it was only a matter of time before that elusive double was landed, with apparently so many big fish in a short section of river. The facts of the matter are very different, since our records show that just two fish accounted for those seven captures. Let us look at the very interesting circumstances surrounding those captures.

In November a bait was taken over a pile of hemp at the bottom of a smooth glide, to be followed by a memorable battle in the dark before a lovely barbel of 8lb 6oz sagged into the landing net. We love eight-pounders; most really epic scraps seem to come from fish of that weight band. Examination of the fish for distinguishing marks revealed a black spot below the left eye and a wart on the lateral line 4 inches from the wrist of the tail, again on the left-hand flank. The right pectoral fin had a very distinct orange coloration in the generally pink background. That fish would now be recognized easily if recaught but, just to make sure, a simple drawing was entered in the diary, outlining these recognition features, together with a record of the fish's weight, time and place of capture, bait used, and so on. It is dangerous to rely on memory. If you are going to base your future angling strategy on anything other than hard documentary evidence, you risk making wrong decisions. In our cases, as we are middle-aged, memory is not as reliable as it once was anyway.

A week after that capture, a lovely slack-line bite in a run above the shallows produced another superb fish of 8lb 2oz. The first thing looked for was the black spot below the left-eye. There was none, and

110

An easily identified Bristol Avon fish weighing 11lb 1oz.

therefore it could be seen straight away that this was a different barbel from the previous week's fish of 8lb 6oz. The new fish was then examined for any identification marks, which revealed an extra barbule at the rear right of the mouth, a wart below the lateral line and immediately above the vent, and a very pronounced bold black line across the lower lobe of the tail. These details were recorded as before.

Over the following weeks, both fish were recaptured twice, the first one at weights of 8lb 12oz and 9lb 1oz and the second fish at weights of 8lb 4oz and 8lb 8oz. In both cases the recorded details enabled identification to be 100 per cent positive.

What conclusions can be drawn from all those separate captures? First, we know that that stretch of river is not crammed with eight- and nine-pounders, otherwise different fish would have been caught. The baiting programme described in Chapter 3 will elicit a response from all barbel in favourable conditions, and the law of averages would be against continually re-catching the same fish if a large head of fish of that size were present. Second, we could be reasonably sure that no really big fish lived in that stretch of river at the time, because it would have showed up. Again, the baiting programme is the key. When swims are continually baited and rebaited for several hours before being fished, to allow the large fish present to overcome their inherent caution, the biggest fish in the vicinity will be the one feeding most greedily. After all, that is the reason why it is the biggest. It becomes the dominant member of the shoal if you like, and this is the reason why the first hookbait is usually the one taken by this senior citizen. Belief in that fact enabled Trefor and Mick to make the decision to move on to a different stretch of river to search for that double. Had they not known for certain that all the big barbel landed during that period comprised just two individual fish they would possibly have spent considerably more time on that section of river in the misguided belief that the elusive double was just round the corner.

Another example from the Bristol Avon demonstrates a second vitally important aspect of the importance of fish recognition. The capture of a barbel of 5lb 2oz was not a particularly remarkable event in itself, but catching that fish resulted in the capture of several double-figure specimens. Let us see how.

That five-pounder was the first fish from a new stretch of river. It accepted two grains of corn at mid-morning in a fast, shallow swim. Once located, the swim was then baited very heavily and over the following two days barbel of 8lb 5oz and 10lb 4oz were to result – a very gratifying introduction to a new stretch indeed, especially as those early fish were caught in conditions that were far from perfect.

Over the following weeks much searching was carried out over the entire length, and eventually the 5lb 2oz fish turned up again, but a considerable distance downstream of where it was first caught. The three raised black scales on one shoulder were an easily identifiable feature. It was felt that the eight- and ten-pounders which accompanied the five-pounder when it was first caught could reasonably be expected to be in the same vicinity if they were members of the same shoal. That conviction led to this new area being baited heavily, and just after dark on the same evening a super fish of 10lb 12oz was to result. Over the following weeks, no fewer than five double-figure barbel were landed from that new area. The recapture of the five-pounder had proved the significant factor that led to the location of a group of huge barbel. This story is proof of the most positive kind that being able to recognize each individual fish gives us tremendous advantages.

As well as indicating when the time may be right to move on to pastures new, the logging of individual barbel can also provide an unexpected new impetus to a stretch you were contemplating discarding prematurely. However clever we become, the fish can also provide new surprises. Tony's fishing on the Cherwell in the 1989–90 season gives a typical example of this principle. For over three seasons it was felt that the stretch in question contained three different double-figure barbel, one of 10lb 3oz which had been landed in September 1987, a fish of 10lb 10oz which had been landed by a match angler, the description of which meant it was definitely a different fish from Tony's ten-pounder, and a third big barbel of certainly over twelve pounds, which Tony eventually hooked and lost in the summer of 1989. The river, in a normal summer, is low and clear, the barbel responding well to hemp, and no big fish other than the three mentioned had ever been observed feeding.

When Tony eventually landed the biggest fish at 12lb 5oz, the decision was made that, once the missing ten-pounder had been landed, a different stretch would be

The Cherwell twelve-pounder that shows a scarred tail root.

examined. When, therefore, a totally new fish of 11lb 4oz turned up, a fresh surge of interest was created. If one double could hide itself, so could others. A significant factor on the Cherwell still is that, despite frequent recaptures from the present areas, and the increasing incidence of this phenomenon, new fish are still turning up. While that situation exists, anything can happen.

The above example of the first capture of the 11lb 4oz fish is a good example of a phenomenon that ensures that the fishing will never be entirely predictable. On any stretch of river there will exist two distinctly different types of barbel, which we have labelled residents and travellers.

Residents are fish which always show up in the company of the same group of other barbel, and they are usually found in one or two swims, in a fairly short section of river. Circumstances that will alter this are the spawning urge, higher water conditions making the area unsuitable, or intense angling pressure spooking the fish out of their normal haunts.

Travellers, on the other hand, are individual fish which display very nomadic tendencies, wandering over possibly many miles. These fish may be alone or they may temporarily join up with other groups of fish, so the capture of a previously unknown barbel does not necessarily mean that you have located a new shoal of fish.

The 11lb Wensum fish with the unmissable round hole in its dorsal fin.

Only subsequent recaptures of the same barbel will enable you to categorize it accurately. The presence of travellers means that you can never be certain that you have exhausted the potential of any stretch of river. The barbel will always hold a few surprises – and a good thing too! Barbel fishing would be very boring otherwise.

Two more extreme examples will bring this chapter to a close. The average angler may be convinced that the Royalty is bursting at the seams with double-figure barbel, to judge from the regular news reports of such captures. In fact, most of the catches are of just one fish, which comes out at weights from 9lb 12oz to as much as 10lb 6oz. She is a lovely barbel, very responsive to angler's baits, and has provided probably dozens of happy anglers with a personal best. Long may she continue to do so. But there is no doubt that her frequent excursions to the bank have given a very distorted view of the population of big barbel on the Royalty.

There is a similar situation with that famous barbel named Beau which lives in the famous stretch of the Wensum. Again, the uninformed angler could be convinced that the Wensum contains a whole crop of twelve-pound-plus barbel, when in actual fact there are only two confirmed fish of that weight. It is impossible to establish the number of times Beau has been landed, but it must run into dozens. Trefor and Dave Plummer have caught that fish no less than nine times between them, at weights varying between 12lb 2oz and 13lb 6oz. If ever a barbel demonstrated the importance of being able to recognize individual fish, dear old Beau does.

11 Final Success on the Wensum

Tony Miles

Since I first started on the trail of Wensum barbel, in the early eighties, the experience of my many angling friends suggests that about one fish in every seven or eight is likely to be in double figures. At the start of the 1987–88 season, that statistic was being totally defied by my own catches. They were remarkable in that not only had I not taken a double-figure barbel in a total of twenty-six fish landed, but they were all in the incredibly narrow weight band of between 6lb 6oz and 8lb 12oz. Catching that elusive Wensum double had become something of an obsession. I was to come agonizingly close to that ambition during my first trip that season, in July.

Following unseasonal heavy rain, the river was high in summer flood, heavily coloured, and perfect for barbel to feed avidly, day and night. On the first night of my trip all my efforts to present my meat baits to barbel were frustrated by eels. They were prolific everywhere, and although I fished through to the early hours of the morning those tackle-tangling horrors were all that I managed to catch. I hate catching eels at the best of times, but after landing the eighth I was feeling murderous. Woe betide the next eel that took my bait!

On the second night I was forced to use huge chunks of meat in an effort to defeat the eel problem, and to a large extent it worked. I still experienced plucks in every swim I fished, but most of them I could safely ignore. The size of bait I was using meant that most of the eels could only nibble the corners away, giving barbel at least a fighting chance of taking the bulk of the hookbait. At last, just before midnight, there was that heart-stopping lunge on the rod top that heralds the arrival of a barbel, and several pulsating minutes later I was admiring an unmarked fish that had beaten my Wensum best by the grand total of two ounces, weighing in at 8lb 14oz. I was very pleased at that capture, but less than an hour later that pleasure had turned to despair.

Fate has a habit occasionally of playing cruel tricks. Soon after my arrival at the Wensum I had realized that I had left all my favourite Au Lion d'Or hooks in my garage at home, and had been forced to revert to a size 4 in another pattern, a very popular specialist hook but one which I had never used before in the larger sizes. That was shortly to prove a very significant factor.

At 1 a.m. on my sixth visit of the night to the Copse swim, I at last had a strong pull and hooked a very large barbel. Soon after I had made contact with the fish it turned over on the surface, and in the moonlight I could clearly see that it was definitely a double. I am almost certain that it was one of the twelve-pounders the river contains.

For a while, although the barbel fought hard, it did nothing really alarming, keeping all the time in relatively open water. Twice it had been almost close enough to net, but it was obviously tiring fast and I had no worries that it would be landed. The fish made one last despairing run downstream, under the large overhanging willow. For the first yard or two, I let the clutch do its work, and then gently applied finger pressure to the spool to stop the fish and turn it. In this I was successful and then, with the barbel coming back upstream towards me, and only modest tension on the line, the hook pulled out. I was absolutely devastated. That fish had been played perfectly. At no time had I anything but total control over the proceedings and yet I had still lost the fish of a lifetime. It could only be sheer bad luck, I thought, though I could not think of the last time I had lost a barbel by an Au Lion d'Or pulling out.

To make a mistake once is understandable, but to repeat the same mistake is unforgivable. You can therefore understand my annoyance with myself when, on the banks of the Wensum a week later, I realized that I still had not put my hook wallet in my box, and was again forced to compromise with the new pattern. I was to get my just rewards for my lack of organization, in the form of two other lost barbel. Another session was almost totally ruined by eels and during two days and nights of hard fishing I had but two chances at barbel, in the long straight below the copse. The first came adrift after a few seconds

A fat eight-pounder.

116

and then, at about 2 a.m. I struck the hook home into another barbel that very obligingly showed itself in the early stages of the fight. Again I had no problems whatever until I was forced to stop the barbel from making the sanctuary of a downstream raft. What happened next bore an uncanny resemblance to the events of the previous week. After exerting heavy pressure to turn the fish from danger, I was slowly bringing it to the net cord when the hook pulled out, again for no apparent reason. I sat down and went through my entire repertoire of swear words, and invented some new ones just for the occasion. To say that I was devastated would be an understatement. To lose two double-figure barbel in successive weeks was bad enough, but to know that it was probably my own fault made it doubly hard to bear. The circumstances of the losses could not be coincidence; they were simply too similar. There had to be something about the hooks that made them loosen their grip in a fish's mouth under pressure, leading to a very insecure hookhold thereafter. Never again would I forget my Au Lion d'Ors. It had been a lesson learned the hard way.

Before my next trip to the Wensum, several weeks later, I had a problem to solve. The eels had been driving me crazy, taking even corn baits, and I gave a lot of thought to creating an eel-proof bait, if such a thing existed, large enough to be used conveniently on a big hook after dark. The only bait on which I had suffered no eel interference was hair-rigged hempseed, and so I decided to make a large bait based on hemp. My first version used dry ground seeds mixed with wheat gluten, baby milk powder, and a little synthetic hemp flavouring, formed into a stiff paste with water. Later on I replaced the ground hemp and flavouring with cooked hemp crushed into a slurry, mixing the paste with the water used for boiling the hemp.

In the afternoon of 3 September I pre-baited half a dozen swims in the normal way, with six bait droppers apiece of hempseed, each dropper-load containing one cherry-sized lump of my new bait. As darkness approached, I baited my size 4 Au Lion d'Or with a chunk of paste the size of a walnut, and swung it out gently to rest on the bait carpet in my favourite Copse swim. With a new bait, it was important for my confidence that I should achieve early success, and that is exactly what happened. Admittedly, it was not a barbel that took the bait after only about a minute, but a four-pound chub was all the encouragement I required. The bait worked; that was all I needed to know.

Half an hour later the Betalight again dipped suddenly and the line tightened over my finger, as a barbel powered away with the bait. Two or three minutes later, a 6½-pounder was being slipped back in the shallows – not a big fish by any standards, but one that was immensely satisfying. At the end of that session I had taken two more barbel, of 6lb 9oz and 6lb 2oz, with no sign of a bite from an eel on the new hemp paste. I had just had the four positive indications from the barbel and chub. An interesting fact was that I had taken two of the three barbel from the Copse swim on the bait, and had reverted for about ten minutes to luncheon meat as an experiment. During those minutes there were several sharp raps on the rod top from eels, and when I carefully wound in the meat I could see several bites out of it. So the eels were certainly active that night, giving me great encouragement that I had actually produced a hookbait that the eels would not touch.

The following night was memorable. The conditions for barbel fishing were a dream, with the river just within its banks and well coloured, but dropping steadily. I had baited as before, and once again the

A syndicate water on the Wensum.

first cast at dusk, in a swim I call the Big Hole, yielded an immediate response in the shape of a barbel of 4lb 6oz, the smallest by far I had ever taken from the river. Far from catching my first double, the barbel were getting progressively smaller.

Two hours later I netted another fish of 7lb 6oz from the Copse, and then came the highlight of my Wensum fishing to date. I was fishing a swim known as the Cattle Drink, on my fifth visit of the night, and for

once decided to stay put in a swim longer than usual. There is no logical reason for that decision, just an unexplainable instinct. I had been sitting there quite quietly, for about twenty minutes, when my attention became distracted to the river bridge, about three hundred yards downstream. It is a very high bridge, some thirty feet above the water, and supports a long since dismantled railway line. After the removal of the tracks, the pathway created has become very popular with dog walkers, courting couples and teenagers, and you get used to people crossing backwards and forwards. However, in the bright moonlight something very unusual was occurring.

In the middle of the bridge a man, who appeared definitely at least middle-aged, started to climb through the rails to balance on the narrow outer parapet over the river, which was flowing very strongly with floodwater at that point. After a minute or two he climbed back again, whereupon he removed his coat and shoes before again clambering through to the parapet. Without hesitation, he lowered himself over the edge and began swinging backwards and forwards over the river, hanging on to the parapet by his fingers. I felt sure that I was about to witness a suicide attempt.

Just at that moment I felt a sudden tightening of the line over my finger, and then the rod crashed down towards the water. As I struck the clutch screamed as an obviously big fish began to run very purposefully upstream. After that initial surge, which gave me temporary palpitations when the barbel became lodged in some cabbages for a while, the battle developed into a dogged power struggle. Up and down the fish plodded, not moving fast but refusing to come off the bottom – the kind of stalemate typical of an extra-big barbel. For fully ten minutes my heart was in my mouth and I expected at any minute to feel the awful gut-wrenching sensation of a hook pulling out. But my old faithful Au Lion d'Or did not let me down, and at last the net mesh closed around my prize. I knew I had my double at last.

A few moments later the light from my torch confirmed its weight at 10lb 5oz, and I then had a decision to make about a photograph. I had to set off for home before daybreak, so it was going to be flash or

nothing. Yet I was on my own and all my camera equipment and tripod were in the car, a good threequarters of a mile away. After a few minutes I decided to take the photographs before starting to fish again, and so set off on the long walk to get my gear. Almost an hour later I was ready, though it had taken me some time to figure out the new flashgun I had bought only the previous week, and half a dozen shots were quickly taken and the fish slipped back. You can probably guess what happened. Despite all my care, I still managed to set the camera with the incorrect synchronization for the new flashgun, with the result that all the photographs of my first Wensum double were totally blank. There is no doubt that I could have had better luck with Wensum barbel!

It was only after the barbel had been returned, and I was ready to recommence fishing, that I remembered the man on the bridge. There was no sign of him, and I often wonder how his antics ended. That memorable session was rounded off in the bridge pool itself, where a lovely crease had formed. If the man I had been watching had jumped in he would have landed almost exactly in the spot where I hooked my fourth and last barbel of the night, a hard-fighting immaculate fish of 8lb 11oz, just after midnight.

Although I have taken many more Wensum barbel since that night, including several nine-pounders, that ten-pounder remains my only double from the river. Compared with Trefor's achievements with the extra-big Wensum fish, my own have been modest. Although I catch as many fish in relation to the time I spend on the banks, the bigger barbel have consistently avoided me. For that reason, my solitary ten-pounder has a very special place in my heart. I just wish that I had a photograph of the damn thing!

12 Snags, Hazards and Other Distractions

We have never lost sight of the fact that the reason we go fishing in the first place is for fun and enjoyment, which is not necessarily directly connected with the fish we catch. Just in case you are getting the impression that we always catch big fish, or that nothing ever goes wrong, this chapter should help to redress the balance a little. It is a look at some of the lighter moments in our barbel-fishing careers, moments that are necessary for us in order to keep the seriousness of the fishing in perspective. All the incidents recounted here are fond and priceless memories and, although some of them have appeared in print before, we make no apologies for that. A book on our barbel fishing simply would not be complete without them. To quote Max Boyce, we know the following stories are true, because we were there.

TONY THE WATER SPANIEL

Tony Miles

Trefor's fondest recollection occurred many years ago on the Throop fishery, just upstream of the bypass bridge. We were fishing side by side, with me perhaps thirty yards downstream of Trefor. It was early evening on a lovely autumn day, and the setting sun was an orange ball of fire in the western sky. Eventually, we had our first

bite, and Trefor struck into what was obviously a good barbel. The fish fought well and for several minutes I was an interested spectator as the battle ebbed and flowed. We had set up only one landing net as we were fishing close to one another, and this had been placed between us. Eventually Trefor called out for the net and I rose from my seat to do the honours. As I walked upstream the bright light from the sun was directly in my eyes, with the result that I mistook floating scum in the margins for solid bank. I quite literally walked straight into the river, which at that point was quite a deep hole, with a steady strong current pushing through it. The only thing that did not get entirely soaked was my hat, which gently floated away. Quite seriously, Trefor remarked that I should stop pratting about and get out to net the fish for him. This I duly managed to do, and then I squelched my way back to the car to see if I could rustle up any dry clothing.

The only spare attire available was a tatty old jumper which was full of holes, a pair of lightweight rubber overtrousers and a pair of old carpet slippers. Believe it or not, I resumed fishing dressed that way, with the rest of my clothes drying over a multitude of branches. They were still not dry when we packed up to go for something to eat, so I accompanied Trefor into a Bournemouth restaurant still dressed the same way. I tell you, some of the looks I received that night were priceless.

Another example of my water spaniel inclinations occurred on my first trip to Ibsley. I had just arrived for a week's fishing, and had not even got as far as putting a rod together. As I walked the bank on an initial reconnaissance, I came to an interesting near-bank streamer bed. I edged forward for a better look into the water, until I was standing on a large tussock of grass right on the edge of the river. Without warning, the tussock gave way and in the blink of an eye I was wallowing in chest-deep water. 'How unfortunate!' is what I think I said.

And what about last summer on the Cherwell? In the afternoon of the day I was eventually to lose the twelve-pound barbel, when I had my daughter Jacqui with me, the first fish I caught was a chub of just over four pounds. Rather than put it back by dropping it over the high bank, Jacqui and I walked two hundred yards to the shallows, where I could show her how to do it properly. I was very serious as we waded out to mid-river with the fish, and explained about releasing the fish gently with its head pointing upstream. The chub swam away strongly and then I went to walk back to the bank. The trouble was, my right foot had become wedged between two stones, and when I tried to walk it did not move. This resulted in me losing my

Barbel spotting!

balance, and I crashed face down in eighteen inches of water. I thought that Jacqui was going to wet herself laughing. Even now, she occasionally shouts 'Timber' and has a fit of the giggles.

Later that summer I was nearly in the river again, but this time I merely ended up speaking in a high voice for a few days. One of the most reliable barbel swims involved fishing off quite a high, sloping bank, which, in times of rain, is extremely slippery. On the night I caught my eleven-pounder, about an hour later, I had another good pull, which resulted in my foul-hooking a decent barbel, which quickly came off. As I struck and climbed to my feet on that very wet night I completely lost my footing, landing flat on my back on the sloping wet clay, which acted like a child's slide. Quite out of control, I shot down the slope towards the edge of the high bank, only to be stopped with a jolt when my rod rest jammed between my legs. That was an anxious moment, I can tell you! I must have made a comical sight that evening, with my legs dangling over the river, face contorted in agony, and arms desperately flailing to find a grip on something solid.

My favourite incident occurred one August on the Wensum. I had climbed high up one of the trees overlooking the Copse swim for a better look at a group of barbel which were feeding over the mid-river gravel. A local angler was on the bank beneath me at the time, and we carried on a conversation as I edged my way along a large branch over the river. Suddenly, I lost my balance and toppled off the branch. As I fell, I instinctively grasped out for a hand-hold and clutched the branch immediately underneath me. My momentum was such that I swung under the branch like a monkey and ended up sitting on top of it. Nonchalantly pretending that I had meant it all along, I shinned down this new

support and soon stood alongside my companion. The look on his face was one of total amazement. He was obviously very impressed.

THE ACROBATIC HORSE

Tony Miles

One of the most comical sights I have seen while barbel fishing on the Cherwell involved a cute but very fat little pony and a nesting pair of swans. The two swans were going about their business on the opposite bank, with the female squatting on her nest and the male fussing around in the margins.

Their nest was adjacent to a shallow area where livestock come down to drink, but the animals have first to negotiate a very steep bit of bank before they can get to the water. Several sheep had fallen in the river at this point over the years, and some had drowned.

The little pony waddled up to the edge of the steep bank and stood there weighing up the options. Obviously he wanted a drink and he cautiously began picking his way down the slope. He had not progressed more than a few feet when his front legs buckled under him and he did a forward gambol down the bank, landing almost on top of the swans' nest. In an instant there was pandemonium, with swans hissing, the horse neighing, and feet, feathers, mud, bits of swans' nest and water flying in all directions. It was a hilarious sight for a few seconds until all the combatants had sorted themselves out, and eventually the pony scrambled back up the bank with damage inflicted on nothing but its dignity.

THE ROYALTY BEAGLE

Trefor West

I love dogs, and have the greatest admiration for their loyalty as well as enjoying their company. My current best friend (she does not answer me back) is Jodie the beagle, ten years old now and, like the rest of us who are middle-aged, pleasantly plump. My wife Kath puts it more simply: 'Jodie is', she says, 'one fat dog.'

The Royalty fishery has its share of dog walkers, and feeding a canine companion a lump of luncheon meat is part and parcel of Royalty fishing. I am a sucker for a wagging tail. It is amazing how much power there is in a lump of meat; just one can win you a four-legged friend for life. The Royalty beagle, however, is a friend I do not need.

I was searching my favourite swim at the bottom of the Trammels, hoping for the third bite of the day. Two six-pounders from the weirpool had fired my interest and enthusiasm to fever pitch. My concentration was disturbed suddenly by the sight of a beagle hurtling towards me at full pelt, its ample ears outstretched and flapping in the breeze. I put the rod down, as the beagle was obviously intending to greet me both enthusiastically and at a tremendous pace. Reaching into my bait pouch, I offered the dog a cube of meat. Firmly ignoring my command to sit, the black-and-tan beagle streaked past my outstretched

A nice seven-plus specimen from the Royalty.

hand with nothing more than a contemptuous look at the morsel he was being offered. Screeching to a halt by my tackle box, he had flipped the lid off my bait box in an instant. Evidently the bait container sitting on the grass at the side of my tackle box was the reason why the dog was in such a hurry, and before I even realized what was happening he had grabbed a whole tin of luncheon meat and was making off with it across the field at the same scorching pace at which he had arrived.

My despairing dive at the thief was a pathetic affair, certainly not worth the energy it consumed, and I missed by a mile. The dog was long gone. My shouts of 'Here boy' were about as effective as the dive, and as I watched him consume the entire tin of meat in about forty seconds flat, a safe twenty yards from me, I could cheerfully have wrung his neck.

I soon saw the funny side of the incident. The beagle knew exactly what he had to do, and I wondered how many other anglers had fallen foul of this bankside felon. That afternoon, on the banks of the Royalty, I was mugged by a bloody beagle!

THE LAUGHING LABRADOR

Tony Miles

Another incident from the Cherwell I shall never forget occurred before I had taken my first double-figure fish from the river. I had located four fish one morning in a near-bank gravel run, and after two fruitless weeks trying for them with sweetcorn, I had decided to fish with a small swimfeeder full of maggots, with a bunch of casters as hookbait. First, though, I had to get the fish feeding confidently, and I spent many hours patiently baiting the swim with hemp, maggots and casters. I intended to

introduce my first hookbait in early evening, when the barbel would have had plenty of time to settle into a confident feeding routine. During the day I became more and more excited. I had several times seen a very big fish on my observation trips to the swim, and thought that my approach guaranteed success. My heart was therefore in my mouth as I eventually crept into position behind the willowherb and gently swung out my terminal rig. Seconds later there was a black flash over my shoulder and an enormous labrador landed with a crash in the very spot where my bait had landed. After a few moments of complete mayhem in the swim, which probably came close to giving every barbel in the vicinity an instant cardiac arrest, the labrador stood at my side, the feeder firmly clamped in his jaws, with what appeared as a great silly grin on his face. As he then proceeded to shake water all over me and tip over my box of maggots, the sweet young thing who had appeared behind me said, 'Don't mind him, he's always being playful.' Several more colourful descriptions had already occurred to me.

THE SEVERN SETTER

Trefor West

I remember my father saying to me that it's not a fool who makes a mistake, but a fool who repeats the same mistake. After the incident of the Royalty beagle, you would have thought I would have learned my lesson, but on a different venue with a different breed of dog I made the same mistake again.

This time it was a beautiful red setter which lives in one of the cottages at Ironbridge on the Severn that I found irresistible. The tail wagged and the first lump of meat disappeared down that cavernous throat without touching the sides.

At first the dog was quite content to sit quietly at my side and await more titbits. Eventually, however, he obviously became dissatisfied with my feeding rate and changed his tactics. He started to whine, quietly at first but steadily building up the volume until he was howling like a werewolf. Not only that, the howls were interspersed with deafening barking, with the dog jumping up and down in an uninhibited frenzy. To make matters worse, setters are renowned for producing large quantities of saliva and the dog was now foaming at the mouth, scattering profuse amounts of froth over everything in the im-mediate vicinity. My clothing and tackle were lathered in the stuff, as was anything else within a radius of five yards.

Another meat cube would calm him down for a few minutes and then the whole performance would start all over again. The trouble was that after each cube of meat the amount of saliva would increase, and it was not long before the foaming reached snow-storm proportions.

The answer to my dilemma came to me in a flash of blinding inspiration. It was time to move swims and introduce the lovely doggy to Mick Nicholls! After all, that's what friends are for – to share experiences with. As I left them to get acquainted, Mick said, 'Thanks, pal'.

A mini battler from the Severn.

'DON'T WORRY ABOUT THE DOG'

Tony Miles

In the last week of the season just ended I was spending a few days on the Dorset Stour, and after dark I decided on a few hours' barbel fishing at a free stretch of river that is used as a public park. There is probably about a mile of bank available, and it is popular with dog walkers.

It was getting quite late, perhaps 11 p.m., and I was sitting quietly, attention focused on my Betalight. I was miles away. Suddenly I became aware of a presence a fraction behind my right ear, and turned round quickly to come face to face with a big black rottweiler. As I had moved quickly, it curled its lip back in a snarl, no more than inches from my own face. I was not happy! Just then, a female voice came out of the blackness: 'Don't worry about the dog, he always gets a bit nervous in the dark. He'll only pounce if you move.' That, of course, was a great comfort. Besides, it is quite difficult to move when you are rigid with fear. If the dog was nervous, what the hell was I? On a serious note, if it had been a child fishing that night, who had become afraid and started to run, that dog could have inflicted some appalling injuries. That stupid woman was completely irresponsible to have that dog off a leash, and I told her so in no uncertain terms.

THE MAD MARE

Tony Miles

This story goes back to my first-ever trip to the Dorset Stour, when I was staying on the caravan park above Iford bridge with three friends.

In the first large meadow below the caravan field there were several horses, and one day my friend Ken decided to feed them on a sliced loaf he had taken along for the purpose. Within minutes of our starting to fish, Ken had got the bread out and, before long, he had a large black mare and her foal taking slices out of his hand. They both scoffed that bread as though they had not seen food for a week, and it was not long before Ken was left with just the empty wrapper.

That mare just did not seem to understand that all the bread was gone. As Ken tried to concentrate on his fishing, the mare became more insistent, nuzzling in Ken's back, each nuzzle being slightly rougher than the last. Suddenly, the mare seemed to go wild and started to charge round the field, kicking her heels in the air.

Discretion being the better part of valour, I moved myself and my tackle over a fence out of harm's way, and eagerly watched to see how Ken would handle the situation. He was, after all, the son of a farmer in Warwickshire.

It soon became apparent that Ken's expertise with animals did not extend to horses, as the mare was getting madder than ever, rearing and snorting very alarmingly. Ken obviously came to the same conclusion as I did and set off in a mad dash to the stile, with the horse in close pursuit. Just in time, Ken dived over the hedge and landed in an undignified heap at my feet. Deprived of its playmate, the mare did no more than gallop back to Ken's tackle and kick the lot into the river.

As I said to Ken, 'Fancy giving a thoroughbred horse bread without jam on it!'

THE PHANTOM SHEEP

Tony Miles

Not long after I had met my old mate Merv Wilkinson, he was doing his level best to get me stuck into my first barbel, and our first joint sorties were to the upper Thames, where Merv had taken several nice fish.

We arrived one morning well before dawn, in one of the densest fogs I have ever attempted to fish in. It was so bad that it took us three times longer than normal to find the river. With only a couple of yards' visibility in any direction, and no landmarks in the middle of an open field to guide us, we were for a time hopelessly lost.

Presently we came to a low hedge that Merv recognized, and slowly we made our way alongside it, Merv keeping about three yards ahead of me. Even at that range he was nothing more than a murky outline in the gloom. Suddenly, there was a yell and he vanished. All of a sudden there were the sounds of galloping hooves all round me. What on earth was going on? It was several minutes before I bumped into Merv again; he was vainly trying to regain his composure. Apparently, in the dark and fog, he had tripped over a sheep that was lying on the ground, startling the animal. It had jumped to its feet in fright with the result that Merv landed on its back, and it then took off like a racehorse with Merv hanging on for grim death. I tell you, it startled me. I cannot imagine what it did to Merv.

A gorgeous upper Thames barbel swim.

127

THE OWL AND THE PUSSYCATS

Trefor West

It was one of those nights when the darkness was absolute. I was fishing the big pool at Berrington on the upper Severn near Atcham. The pool is surrounded by large trees and is in complete isolation from all the sights and sounds of civilization. The darkness is further accentuated by the foliage from the encircling trees, and the pool is not a place to be at night if you are of a nervous disposition. That was no problem to me, as I had spent half my life fishing after dark – much of that time in gloomy, sinister places – without anything untoward occurring. Tonight was going to be different.

A fish extracted from the edge of the snag in the middle of the pool, just after dark, fuelled my anticipation. Maybe tonight I would hook the huge barbel that I had seen several times in the swim over the previous days. I was wrapt in concentration, and then the lead moved. It was a definite bite, but all my confident strike met with was thin air. Cursing to myself, I reeled in the terminal tackle, wondering if I had just blown my chance at the big fish. As I rebaited, the rod was held loosely in the crook of my arm, pointing skywards, the Betalight glowing brightly in mid-air. Suddenly the rod took on a new life all of its own, plunging around with tremendous ferocity. I looked up into the intense blackness and all I could see was a grotesque white phantom attacking me. It was only feet away from my face, and in a split second a contented barbel angler had been transformed into a mass of quivering jelly.

Whatever the apparition was seemed determined to take the top six inches of my rod, and then I slowly made out great white wings, just as huge glaring red eyes stared straight into mine. It was then that I realized that a barn owl had seized the Betalight, and for a while I had visions of a great hooked beak and wickedly curved talons sliding down the rod to attack my face.

The entire incident probably took only a

few seconds, before the owl realized its error of judgement and disappeared into the darkness as silently as it had arrived. During those seconds, however, my tranquil mental state had been damaged beyond repair. Future sessions at the pool would see the rod top equipped with a coil of barbed wire, to deter any future nocturnal attackers.

All my angling encounters with cats over the years have fallen into the amusing category, with the notable exception of one incident on the banks of the River Wensum.

I was fishing the famous fallen tree swim, again after dark, but with a bright moon throwing the countryside into brilliant relief. I noticed a movement on the far bank

and after a moment or two my eyes focused on a cat creeping through the grass. There are quite a few wild cats on the banks of the river near Norwich, living on their wits. Obviously, this one was stalking something and eventually it sprang on its prey, probably a mouse or vole. There were a few squeaks from the tiny victim and then an ominous silence returned.

A few moments later I noticed another movement opposite me, a few yards away from the cat, which was preoccupied in devouring its hard-won meal. I realized that the hunter was now the hunted as I saw the form of a fox dart forward. The cat was taken completely unawares, so lightning-fast was the attack. I could only be a horrified spectator as the fox fastened its jaws

A lovely 11lb 10oz Bristol Avon fish.

round the cat's throat, and I will never forget the blood-curdling screams of pain and fright as the cat fought for its life. For several minutes that fox shook the cat viciously backwards and forwards, with the unfortunate victim slowly losing the unequal fight. The squealing rose to a deafening pitch as the cat's death throes echoed down the once peaceful Wensum valley, and then a merciful conclusion came to the affair. Suddenly, the struggling ceased, and the fox trotted off into the undergrowth with his prize, completely unaware that his role in this isolated example of nature in the raw had been witnessed by human eyes.

There is a remarkable cat on the banks of the Bristol Avon, with which Mick Nicholls and I have had several encounters.

Our first meeting with this feline left us very puzzled until we grasped the answer to the riddle. We were walking the river in the close season, spotted a pure-white cat sitting in a tree fifty yards or so upstream, and remarked on it in passing. The cat disappeared at our approach and we thought no more about it. Only a minute or so later,

there was the cat about fifty yards away again, but this time on the opposite bank. How had it managed to go down river about a hundred yards, cross it, and come back up the opposite bank in such a short time? It was a mystery, and Mick Nicholls was no help. His blank expression said it all.

Mike Stevens said that it was easy to explain. Wiltshire cats, he said, were renowned for being the fastest in the world, and what we had just witnessed was nothing unusual. Mick Nicholls uttered a one-word reply, one that signifies disbelief, and at that very moment a pure-white cat shot out from the long grass at our feet. There are two identical pure white cats!

My mistake was in tossing the white cat a piece of luncheon meat in the first place. Now, every time we fish that stretch of river, one of those cats miraculously appears from nowhere, demanding to be fed, miaowing constantly and rubbing itself against our waders.

The cat soon realized where the meat cubes were kept – a small bait pouch at my waist – and one day the situation became

Fiddlers – a Royalty hotspot.

totally farcical, as the cat leapt on to my lap and buried its head in the pouch, gulping meat down as fast as it could chew. Bite detection was now quite difficult, to say the least, with the cat balancing precariously on my lap, with its face buried in the bait pouch and its tail and rear end in my face. It's a tom cat, by the way. Funny how you notice these minor details!

Despite the rod waving all over the place, which was made even worse by my hysterical laughter, I still detected a bite. As I struck, the rod went one way and the cat another, with the rod butt fetching it a departing thump up the backside. The barbel surged away, making the clutch sing, and at that moment the cat began clawing its way up my waders again. Nothing was

going to stop it getting its head back in that pouch. As I played the barbel the cat hung on for grim death, and by now I was laughing uncontrollably. Talk about the Benny Hill fishing show!

Eventually, and unbelievably, I actually managed to land the barbel, and I am now contemplating whether to claim the Bristol Avon white-cat-on-your-lap river record.

THE CRAFTY CORMORANT

Tony Miles

This is another story from the Dorset Stour, and undoubtedly the episode is

131

among the most startling of my angling career. I was fishing at Longham, using the swimfeeder, and was really struggling for bites. I had managed an early three-pound barbel and lost another, but apart from that the fishing was slow. I did, however, have a succession of small taps which at first I attributed to small dace. I began to wonder whether they might be caused by particularly cautious barbel after all, and decided to strike at the next indication, no matter how insignificant it appeared. Presently, the quivertip twitched again and moved forward about half an inch, and I struck. Initially there was quite feeble resistance, but then the rod really buckled over. Something powerful was fighting like crazy, and I scrambled to my feet, congratulating myself on a skilful bit of angling. Suddenly, right under my feet, the water erupted and a great black apparition flew out of the water, heading straight for my face. I nearly had a coronary at that moment. What had happened was that a small dace had taken the maggots and the cormorant had attacked the dace as I had struck. Luckily, the bird was not hooked, the dace being held crosswise in its beak, and as it gained height the fish was released. It was ten minutes before I recast. My hands were trembling so much I couldn't fill the feeder.

SELF-CATERING CHAOS

Tony Miles

Whenever we have gone away for a few days' fishing, we have always catered for ourselves, sleeping either in the car or, over the last few years, in our vans. These days, Trefor goes fishing in a converted Honda van while I use a Volkswagen motor caravan – unashamed luxury compared with what we used to put up with.

During the years when we only had our cars, we often used to sleep under our umbrellas alongside convenient hedges, and this resulted in one hilarious night in Dorset. We had been fishing Throop and had just settled down in a quiet country lane when a carload of foreign students screeched to a halt beside us. They spoke very little English, but obviously saw in us two kindred spirits, and before long several bottles of wine had been produced and the party was in full swing. Initially, we attempted to ignore them and vainly tried to get some sleep. It soon became obvious that there was absolutely no chance of that, so we joined in with the merry-making. After about an hour, with all the wine having been consumed, and both Trefor and me feeling the worse for wear, the students all piled back in their car and were soon weaving their way down the lane. It was now about 1.30 a.m.

Again we settled down and closed our eyes. The world started to spin slowly and then I suddenly became aware of a strong light in my eyes.

'What's all this, then?' a gruff voice boomed out.

At that I woke with a start to see two police officers standing over us. In the next few minutes they proceeded to tell me that they did not welcome vagrants in their patch and that we had better be gone at six o'clock in the morning when they would be passing once again.

At that moment Trefor nearly got us arrested. 'That would be ideal,' he said. 'We want to be up at six to go fishing, so if you could give us a shout at about a quarter to six you can have a cup of tea with us before we leave.'

For a while the two officers just looked at each other, and then they burst out laughing and agreed to do as Trefor had suggested. Sure enough, they were back at 5.45 a.m. and they spent about half an hour with us, drinking tea and wolfing down bacon sandwiches. When we finally said our goodbyes we had all become firm friends.

Talking about men in uniform reminds me of a particularly hair-raising night when we were returning from the Thames in my car. It was about midnight, and just outside Oxford we saw a young lady thumbing a lift. It was obvious from her manner that she was quite distressed. After we had picked her up we found out that she was a member of the American Air Force, stationed at Upper Heyford nuclear air base. Apparently she had been taken to a party in Oxford by one of the pilots and been abandoned there. She was already an hour after curfew and terrified of the disciplinary action that might follow if she could not get back until the next morning.

As Upper Heyford only entailed a very minor detour on our way home, we agreed to drop her at the camp gates. Neither Trefor or I had ever met such an embittered woman in our lives before. She was a black girl of twenty years of age and told us of her early life in the Bronx. She had, she said, been forced to kill two men when she was fifteen years of age to defend herself, and that was why she always carried a knife in her handbag. I was now having serious misgivings.

One thing I still do not believe is the fact that there was absolutely no security at the entrance to the base that night, and for a long time neither Trefor nor I realized that we had actually entered a restricted area. It was not until we started to drive past billets and American military vehicles that we realized what we had done. By this time we had made several twists and turns, following the girl's directions, and we were now firmly stuck in a one-way system. Suddenly, she had opened the back door, and, without a word, had scampered away among the buildings, leaving Trefor and

me in the middle of a US nuclear base in the middle of the night without authority. I could think of healthier places to be.

'I tell you mate,' I said, 'if we're caught here now, with no proof of how we came to be here, it's going to be a nasty situation.'

Following the one-way system was obviously going to lead us deeper and deeper into the interior of the base, so I made the decision to turn the car round and attempt to make my way back the way I had come, while praying that we did not meet anything coming the other way. A few hundred yards was negotiated without incident, and then, as I turned a right-hand bend, I came face to face with an armoured car. 'Now we really are in it' was Trefor's contribution to the dialogue.

Keeping as composed as possible, I wound down the driver's window, and seconds later a machine gun was jammed in my right ear. It was then suggested that I 'start talking'. After I had poured out my story, the serviceman, who was on routine camp patrol, obviously believed we were genuine. It was probably something in the tone of my voice – a mixture of sincerity and abject terror. What he said was that he would turn his vehicle round and that we should follow him out of the camp. He did warn us, though, that, should we meet up with any military police, we would be on our own. Naturally, that was very comforting. Luckily, however, there was no further incident, and it was two very relieved barbel anglers who eventually sped away that night.

One of the biggest problems when you are spending a few days in the country is that of getting soaked on the first day and having no means of drying clothes. This can prove to be an expensive problem. Several years ago, on the Royalty, we had fished all day in incessant rain and, despite our waterproofs, the rain had found its way through to our other clothes. I had spares of everything except thermal underwear, whereas Trefor had no spare jumpers with him. We therefore decided to go into Bournemouth, find a launderette, and dry my Damart one-piece suit and Trefor's jumpers in a powerful tumble drier. It is obvious that we do not do the washing at home!

Half an hour later the clothes came out of the machine baking hot, and a totally different size and shape from when they went in. Trefor's jumpers would have quite comfortably fitted King Kong, whereas my Damart underwear set had shrunk to about a third of its original size.

It was that incident that taught us that thermal wear must not be tumble-dried, and so when Trefor got his thermal outer suit soaking wet one day on the Bristol Avon he knew that he could not dry it that way. He soon discovered an alternative. The farmer was burning some rubbish, the fire crackling quite merrily, and Trefor hung the suit on a nearby fence to dry in the warm air. The trouble was that a spark caught it and in a matter of seconds Trefor watched a nearly new garment cremated.

In fact, Trefor showed arsonist tendencies not long after he had first kitted out his van as a fishing home. Cooking his bacon and eggs one morning on his Calor gas stove, he suddenly noticed that the flame was much higher than it should have been. The reason soon became obvious. The curtains were on fire.

Possibly the most annoying thing about self-catering out of a car or van, especially when you are miles from anywhere on a cold day or night, is having to attend to that essential bodily function that is very difficult to perform discreetly. In my case, it has led to two very funny incidents.

Last winter I was spending three days on the Dorset Stour, my van being parked in a quiet country lane, and in the late afternoon I had just finished a meal before resuming my search for a barbel. That old urgent feeling came over me and I pushed my way through the bushes at the side of the road to attend to a call of nature. Hidden from view, and surrounded by foliage, I was soon crouched down, trousers round my ankles, when a young woman came past me from behind, with a dog on a lead. Heaven knows where she sprang from. 'Good afternoon,' she said, appearing to be totally unperturbed by what I was doing, and carried on through the foliage and out towards the road as if nothing untoward was occurring. I could have died of embarrassment.

One night on the Wensum I was again in the same predicament, and was trying to find a private place among all the bracken and fallen trees alongside an overgrown stretch of the river. Eventually I found the right spot and slowly backed under some thick bushes. Crouching once again, I went to shuffle backwards a few inches when, all of a sudden, I felt myself tumble backwards down a very steep slope. With my feet effectively trapped by the trousers round my ankles, I was helpless until I had stopped falling, and eventually I came to rest on my back in the mud at the edge of the river. I must have looked for all the world like a giant baby awaiting its nappy being changed.

Self-catering calls for great attention to detail. Trefor and Mick Nicholls had planned a four-day session together, both staying in Trefor's van. Obviously, a fair bit of planning is involved, what with bait to prepare, food to buy, and so on. It is very easy to forget something and if you are self-reliant for a few days it may not always be convenient to replace the forgotten item. When Mick rang Trefor just before he left home to pick him up, Trefor naturally assumed that Mick had remembered something of vital importance.

'Glad I caught you, mate,' he said, 'but I

thought I better ring in case you forgot the tea cosy.' That's what I call getting your priorities right!

THE LEGEND OF MAD MORETON

Trefor West

Over the years I have met several individuals who could be described as anti-angler. Usually, their anger towards us has been aroused by an anglers' bad behaviour, litter, trespass and other antisocial activities. Unfortunately, the minority of idiots in our ranks often lead to us all being tarred with the same brush.

Perhaps it was a bad experience with an angler that led to the extreme attitude of a certain Wal Moreton, Esq., the wildly eccentric inhabitant of a decrepit old bungalow right on the banks of the River Wensum. Added to his apparent hatred of all anglers is an unpredictable and totally par-

anoid attitude to the world in general. The man has earned his title of 'Mad Moreton' a thousand times over, and to attempt to describe all his antics over the years would require a book of its own. However, the following few tales should help you build up a picture of this most mellow of old English gentlemen.

The old Ford missed me by inches as it screeched to a stop, following which Moreton leapt from behind the wheel shouting obscenities. 'This is my private road,' he screamed, the blood vessels on his forehead swelling as he worked himself into a frenzy. My suggestion that he calm down fell on deaf ears, and in a rage he stormed round to the back of his car, opened the boot and withdrew an axe, which he proceeded to brandish in a most threatening manner. Obviously, it was not his intention to chop firewood.

Quickly, I backed off, as he lurched towards me on very unsteady legs. Luckily for me, his movements are very laboured and awkward, as the result of many injuries

135

Playing a summer Kennet fish.

A flooded Kennet in winter.

sustained in speedway crashes years ago, when he had been a top rider in Norwich. It is rumoured that his obsessive hatred towards the world can be attributed to the steel plate that had to be inserted in his head after a particularly nasty crash on the track.

The profanities continued, the axe waving backwards and forwards really menacingly.

'Look, Wally,' I said, 'the only way you can stop me using this track to get to the river is to stand on guard day and night, and that seems a stupid thing to do. After all, I only want to walk about a hundred yards before going into the field to fish. Why don't you calm down and go up the pub tonight and have a good drink on me?'

The words drink and pub seemed to cool his temper a little, but he still screamed shrilly as he said, 'It's my private road, so it will have to be a really good drink!' With the fiver in his top pocket, he stalked round the back of the car muttering to himself, slammed the boot, lurched back into the driving seat, and with a great grinding of gears screeched off up the track, spraying me with dust and gravel in the process. My first encounter with Mad Moreton was over.

A few weeks later, old Wally was up to his antics again, and this time his eccentricity could have cost me a fortune. I strolled back down to the river after relaxing over a good meal, confident that the huge barbel I had located would surely pick up my hookbait later that evening. All was well with the world. Suddenly my heart missed a beat as I approached my tackle. There was no chair, no landing net, no rod or reel. The seat box was still in position, so I immediately ruled out thieves, who would certainly have taken that as well.

As I got closer, I noticed my chair in the middle of the river, and as I waded out to retrieve it from its watery grave I was disconsolate to find no trace of my net or rod. They would probably be floating towards Norwich by now, and I cursed myself for my stupidity in leaving them on the bank while I had my break back at the van. The gate to the field is normally closed but on this particular day it had been left open to allow access for the farmer's tractor. Of course, it also allowed Mad Moreton to vent his antagonism on my tackle, for I was now sure that was what had happened. Slowly, I wandered downstream in the vain hope that the missing items had simply been hidden in the long grass. Soon I was pleased to see the handle of my landing net bobbing up and down alongside the trees on the opposite bank. Luckily, the mesh had caught in the branches, and after edging out over the river on a thin branch I was just able to grap the handle and retrieve the net.

Soon afterwards I located the £100 carbon rod and irreplaceable Cardinal 54, wedged sideways across a weed raft in midstream adjacent to the bottom bend, several hundred yards away from where I had been fishing. It was the work of a moment to strip off, plunge into the river and retrieve the remainder off my gear, and as I walked back up the field the sense of relief was tremendous. At that moment I just knew that I was destined to catch a huge barbel that night.

Then I saw Wally Moreton watching me from his car, hidden behind the bushes, and that was when I vowed never to leave my tackle unattended on the Wensum again. Seeing that his ploy had proved unsuccessful, he flew into another rage and again screamed off up the track in his long-suffering car, accompanied by the customary cloud of dust and gravel – but not before I had given him the normal sign of displeasure.

The barbel I had promised myself did

indeed keep to the script that night, weighing in at an immensely satisfying 11lb 14oz, and completed an altogether unforgettable session.

On the bank opposite Wally's bungalow, the willow bush cover has long been a favourite holding spot for Wensum barbel. The problem is that if the old fool sees you fishing near his home he throws almighty tantrums, his behaviour becoming more bizarre by the minute. The wonder is that he has not had a heart attack before now. He must have an iron constitution.

After the usual volley of curses and obscenities, and threats of physical assault, Wally's tactics usually involve him dancing up and down on the bank like a giant demented parrot, while hurling rocks and anything else he can lay his hands on into the swim. All of this, of course, is very conducive to good barbel fishing.

If this approach fails to deter the encroaching angler, Wally then goes in to what must surely be his party piece – stripping off down to the most filthy pair of underpants imaginable and launching himself into the river. After a good wash right where you had been fishing, and a non-stop barrage of profanities, Wally departs the scene – along with every self-respecting fish within a hundred yards.

Old Wally Moreton is priceless, and every Wensum angler I know has a tale to tell about the cantankerous old hooligan. Really, he is quite a sad figure, just a lonely old man, if you can possibly ignore the colourful language! Mad Moreton has become part of Wensum barbel fishing folklore, and I know that when he eventually passes on I will certainly miss him. The Wensum will never seem quite the same again.

13 Great Ouse Barbel of the 1990s

Tony Miles

Although I fished a further season on the Cherwell following the events of 1989, (see Chapter 6), taking two more eleven-pounders, no more new big fish turned up and the level of recaptures convinced me that I had enjoyed the best of it and it was time to move on. I had been looking increasingly at my favourite river, the Great Ouse, where reports of good barbel were becoming frequent. I had very little to go

An immaculate eleven-pounder taken in a winter flood.

A 14lb 2oz monster.

on, except that the river was thought to hold good barbel for almost its entire length, excluding the extreme upper and lower reaches. One clue that was to prove very significant arose when I gave an angling club AGM a slide show in 1990, at which I was asked to present an award to an angler who had taken a barbel of over 10lb from a club water. Although I had no intention of jumping in on the fishing, preferring to find my own fish, the venue was earmarked as one to receive attention in the future. In fact, it was a further five years before that was to happen.

The summer of 1991 saw my first session on a very scenic section of the middle river which I knew to contain a reasonable head of barbel, although the potential for very big fish was unknown. Catching a few fish was the first priority – I would worry about the sizes later. During the following three years, I fished dozens of days and nights, walked many miles of bank, both on dry land and in the river, searching for fish and features, and it was a most exciting and rewarding period. Although my first Ouse double had stubbornly eluded me by the summer of 1994, by which time I had taken eleven nine-pounders, I had served an invaluable apprenticeship. I therefore felt that my first Ouse doubles, of 10lb 13oz and 11lb 6oz, in the autumn and early winter of 1994, were just recognition for my efforts.

The close season of 1995 was a time of planning the season to come, plans that included having a look at the section of river that I had first heard of in 1990. There was then an amazing coincidence. My good friend Matt Hayes, with whom I had been trying to organize a fishing trip for some time, rang to see if I fancied a barbel trip to the same section of river. The following week, we met on the banks of this stretch and after only a few minutes we were to spot several giant fish under an old fallen willow. At that time, the stretch was very lightly fished, apart from a couple of regulars, and we had a plentiful choice of swims. That first week, I was to blank, apart from a small chub, but I had the extreme pleasure of photographing a superb fish of 11lb 13oz for Matt – one of the longest barbel I had ever seen. As I drove home after that first trip, my mind was racing. I was convinced that I had found at least two fish that topped 13lb. I could not wait to get back.

The following week, under a fallen willow on the far bank, around which floating weed and algae had accumulated to form a raft, were four barbel. One of the fish was a colossal light-coloured one, then there was a smaller one of about 7lb and two others of around 9lb. I had already decided to use as hook bait Pescaviva red strawberry-flavoured corn, as fish had been seen to spook on the yellow variety the previous week. After an initial baiting of five large handfuls of hemp and two of corn, I fed a dozen or so grains of corn every few minutes for the first half hour before setting up my tackle.

I was using 10lb Trilene XT, the hooklink being 18in of 12lb Drennan braid, to a size 6 Au Lion D'or. I would have liked a longer hooklink, but the cast to the upstream edge of the raft was hampered by a trailing branch. However, I felt confident that patient feeding would draw the fish upstream under the debris and soon I was watching the rod top intently, as my two grains of red corn rested enticingly on the gravel under the upstream edge of the

foliage. To minimize line bites, small pieces of tungsten putty were placed on the main line for four feet above the lead to nail the line to the riverbed, out of harm's way.

About an hour later, I was on my feet, the clutch whining, as a big barbel tried to force its way further under the foliage. As I countered that with maximum sidestrain, there was a horrible grating, and then the fish came free and slowly began to yield to the tremendous pressure I was exerting. Suddenly, it shot from under the raft, after which there were no more anxious moments and soon a lovely barbel folded into the net. It was one I had originally estimated at 9lb, but it turned out to be much bigger than that. Moments later, I was confirming 10lb 8oz, an exciting baptism to my barbel catches on a new stretch of river.

As the morning wore on, heavy overnight rain started to make its presence felt, in the shape of a significant increase in current speed. I was forced progressively to increase lead and by about 2.00 pm it needed an ounce to hold the terminal rig in position. The second bite took me completely unawares. I had lifted the rod from the rest, to dip the line out of the path of floating weed, when it suddenly lunged downstream. An almighty boil erupted under the branches, and again I was off my chair and heaving for all I was worth. The barbel was almost a twin of the first, at 10lb 6oz; this was the first time I had taken two doubles in a day and I was elated.

The next morning dawned bright and sunny, and my first job back at the swim was to look behind the raft. After a short while, two barbel tails slowly backed into the open air. Soon, they were in full view, the little 'un and the monster, as I had mentally christened them. Watching the fish closely for about ten minutes as they came and went under the raft convinced me that they were feeding avidly. At 9.00 a.m., I was to land the little 'un, although little was hardly an apt description of a chunky fish that pulled the needle to 8lb 10oz. This was getting exciting. The only fish left under the raft was the monster, and eventually, at 11.00 a.m., the rod shot off the rest. As I struck, there was an explosion of spray under the raft, an almighty pull, and then the line went limp. I experienced that terrible empty feeling, and when I checked the hook, my worst fears were realized. The hook point was turned right over. I had just foul-hooked the monster. My chances of success today now looked bleak indeed. Knowing that I now had to rest the swim, I steadily fed with corn grains for several hours. During this feeding, however, the big fish sat steadfastly at the rear of the raft, and it was obvious I had to get a bait to the fish, as it was not about to come to me.

At the gravel shallows I did some experiments with a hook, using varying amounts of rig foam. What I wanted was a hook that floated on its own, but just held bottom with two corn grains in place so that it would easily follow the dictates of the current. Having achieved that aim, it was time to put the second part of the plan into operation. I had calculated that the head of the barbel was 9ft downstream of the closest point I could land my tackle and so I measured a 9ft hooklink of braid, attached the buoyant hook, and then carefully coiled the link around two fingers until the whole link was no more than 6in long. It was then tied tightly with PVA string, the theory being that when the PVA melted, the flow would act on the buoyant hook to unravel the hooklink and allow the corn to trundle straight into the barbel's mouth. It sounded feasible, but would it work? Ten minutes after the cast I had my answer as the rod wrenched over, and I at last joined battle with the leviathan.

The fight went much as it had with the two ten-pounders the previous day, the fish continually trying to wrap me up in the branches, but the tackle was sound, the pressure from me relentless, and eventually the barbel yielded, and shot upstream past me, but into clear, snag-free water. At that point the battle was won, and I was soon heaving the barbel of my dreams on to the bank. As it lay there on the net, I almost went to pieces, I was shaking so much. But eventually I carefully zeroed my scales with the wet weigh sling and placed the gigantic barbel into it for the moment of truth. When the needle settled on 13lb 8oz I knew that one of my longest held angling dreams had come true. That day, alone on the banks of a beautiful river, the summer sun burning my back, I had found my own private heaven.

After several more big fish that season, I was naturally itching to return at the start of the 1996 season, and my second session turned out to be one of the most incredible day's barbel fishing I've ever experienced. When I arrived, I found that I had been beaten to the swim I fancied by Adrian Busby, whom I had first met when he photographed my thirteen-pounder and who has now become a good friend. As we stood talking and looking into his swim, we could see that there were six fish in residence, all huge. It hardly seemed possible, but the smallest could have been 11lb and the biggest was just mind-blowing.

Less than an hour later, I was back with him, photographing a magnificent fish of 13lb 3oz, and I could tell by the way he was soaked to the chest that he'd had to go in after it. Incredibly, despite the commotion, the remaining five fish still fed, apparently unconcerned, which was confirmed a short while later when Adrian pulled out an estimated twelve-pounder.

It was midday when Adrian shouted that he had just netted another one and when we confirmed a weight of 12lb 8oz, I realized that this was the largest barbel brace I had ever seen. It was then that he told me

The roots of this old willow produced my first-ever Ouse barbel.

that he had to leave at 2.00 p.m. for a prior commitment. 'Why don't you move in when I go?', he said. 'The three fish left are still feeding.' Although I had grave reservations about whether any more bites could possibly materialize after the commotion Adrian had created in the swim that morning, the three fish still present were too big to ignore. Consequently, at a little after 2.00 p.m., I moved my gear as Adrian left. His departing words were prophetic. 'Ring me if you do any good', he said. 'I'll be back home after four.' I tackled the swim using my adjustable hair rig, on 2lb nylon, with a quarter-inch hair, on to which were super-glued two corn grains, giving as subtle a presentation as mounting a bait on a tiny hook. To disguise the size 6 Au Lion D'or, I wound a twelve corn grain stringer around

it, the theory being that when the PVA melted, it would be buried under a little mound of corn. At around 3.45 p.m., the rod crashed round, and for a few vital seconds, the battle was temporarily stale-mated, with my refusing to give line and the barbel refusing to yield. But then I felt the fish give a little, and knew that, barring a stupid mistake on my part, the fight was as good as over. With the fish reluctantly bowing to my relentless pressure, I exerted even more and managed to heave it from under those far bank branches and into the open water of midriver, where I caught my first glimpse of it. It was massive. It was now a question of keeping a cool head, and about five minutes after first setting the hook, this tremendous barbel rolled into the net, a fish that subsequently proved to

The middle Ouse carrying eight feet of floodwater.

be three ounces short of a personal best, at 13lb 5oz. An hour later, just as Adrian had returned to photograph my fish, I was in again, and when we subsequently weighed another double at 10lb 11oz we realized that the fishing was entering the realms of fantasy. The swim had now produced four doubles, one lost, and the fish that remained was the biggest of the lot!

That evening, I was not to discover quite how big that final fish was. Although I did hook it, I had cast just a little too close to the snag, and it was immovable from the word go. Eventually, I was forced to pull for a break, retrieving a straightened hook instead, and knew that I would never rest until I had landed that unseen monster.

A week later, I stood in the early morning sunlight watching fish in the swim, my initial reaction being one of intense disappointment, as the swim now contained a dozen average barbel, with no big ones. And then a sudden flash to my left caught my eye, and I turned to see an enormous barbel drift out from under a streamer clump and then meander in leisurely fashion downstream, to disappear under the foliage of the branches. Immediately, I knew that this was the fish I was after.

With lesser fish in residence, I felt that at least two hours' feeding were necessary before placing a hook bait, to allow the big one to exert feeding dominance, but it was late morning before a hook bait was introduced. I didn't have long to wait, however.

With the sun blazing down, the rod suddenly took on a life of its own and plunged round. I struck and heaved all in one movement and, following an impressive swirl under the branches, the barbel lost the battle with a fatal error of judgement. Instead of going full tilt for the snag, it shot downstream into a thick bed of streamer, but away from those all-important roots. Once away from danger, a combination of heavy pressure and side-strain kept the fish kiting into midriver, and then he emerged from the streamer, heading upstream quite fast. That was when I saw the full length of the barbel for the first time and at that moment my heart nearly stopped. It was indeed a giant amongst barbel.

In truth, I was never in any serious danger of losing that fish, although the unexpected can never be ruled out until it is in the net. When I eventually heaved the fish on to the bank, and peeled back the folds of mesh, the sight that greeted me will never fade. There, glistening in the summer sun, was one awe-inspiring barbel. Minutes later, weigh sling dampened and scales zeroed, I faced the moment of truth and watched in fascination as the needle raced round the dial. When it stopped at 14lb 7oz it was a truly special moment.

A year to the day, in July 1997, I was back at the stretch, but this time fishing a swim containing a big head of fish feeding avidly on hemp, corn and maggots. This time, I could not specifically target a big fish and so I was perhaps a little lucky in the size of barbel that did take the bait. I will never forget the bite, the rod went round a yard,

I'll swear. As soon as I struck, I knew that here was something really special, as it fought deep and slow but with great power, a real brute of a thing that just did not want to yield. Because of extensive weeds and snags, I did not allow the fish an inch of line. But none could be won either, and for several minutes, we were stalemated. Anglers have often commented on how hard I play fish, but my response is always that I prefer to lose a fish in the fight than have to pull for a break on a snag. For a few minutes, the barbel strained for tree roots, with me equally determined to stop him, and then it suddenly gave up the effort, rolled and came back under the rod top. At that moment I saw an incredible depth of flank and knew that once again I was playing a truly awesome barbel. Moments later, it was all over, and another monstrous barbel graced my landing net.

Since my capture of that particular fish, which weighed 14lb 2oz, it has gone on to earn its rightful place in barbel fishing history, having been caught several times at over 15lb and to date three times at 16lb plus, the biggest a mind-boggling 16lb 12oz.

So there we have a very brief résumé of the highlights of my Ouse barbel fishing through the 1990s. At the time of writing, November 1998, I am about to begin a winter campaign for another big fish, and there may soon be other exciting tales to tell. But whatever the future holds, the last few years are a treasure trove of wonderful memories. All the soakings, the blanks, the waiting, the miles of walking, were all forgotten in moments of pure elation. I wouldn't change a minute of it.

14 Double Top

Trefor West

The swim had brilliant credentials, in that twenty-odd barbel had been taken from it the previous season. A few four-pound fish had been caught, along with the odd six- or seven-pounder, but it was eight-pound-plus specimens in the main that Mick Nicholls and I came to expect. There is nothing in fishing that I love more than catching eight-pound-plus barbel.

As well as several eight-pounders, the swim produced four different nines and two double-figure fish of 10lb 4oz and 10lb 10oz – a superb swim. The feeling that a twelve-pound barbel from this small section of river was a distinct possibility, in our first season on the Bristol Avon, ensured that our enthusiasm never waned. Even repeat captures of several of the eight-pounders and two of the nines did not deter us, as we felt it highly possible

A typical holding area.

that a lone, exceptionally large barbel could well join the resident fish towards the back end of the season.

Mick and I understandably fished it very hard, as we both felt that this was the most consistent area we had located in our preliminary investigations of the river. As the season drew to a close, our hard work having paid off handsomely, we were already looking forward with keen anticipation to the season to come.

As it always does, the close season absolutely flew by, and once more life had a purpose as the magic day of 16 June came upon us. These days, I do not fish much in the early part of the season, preferring to work long hours in the summer months, thus placing myself in a sound financial position to be able to fish when and as long as I choose in the autumn and winter months, when the barbel fishing is much more consistent. Being self-employed, I am able to control my own destiny, and therefore my barbel-fishing trips in the latter half of the season can always be timed to coincide with ideal water and weather conditions. Although I love the summer fishing, there is no doubt that the long summer days can drag. As often as not, the few hours of half-light and darkness is the only time you can reasonably expect big-barbel activity.

I did, however, have a short trip to the Bristol Avon at the opening of the new season, both catching a few nice barbel and having the opportunity to reacquaint myself with the river. After that initial visit, it was a further six weeks before I returned, for a two-day session. This was as much to keep tabs on the place as it was to fish.

As I expected, the river was very low and clear, the bankside vegetation having grown four feet since June. I knew that the low water level would make life very difficult, and that my only chance of catching barbel would be to search in localized swims with plenty of cover. Overhanging bushes and trees, or anything else that sheltered the fish from the strong sunlight, would be where my efforts would be concentrated.

There are several swims of this type on the first section of river I visited, with twenty- or thirty-yard lengths of hawthorns forming bankside canopies low enough to accumulate rubbish rafts around their lower branches. I knew that one particular swim would contain the bulk of the barbel that Mick and I had located in that area.

As I approached the swim my heart sank, as it became all too horribly obvious that we had been blessed with a visit from the Wessex Water Authority. Every single bush and tree that could possibly offer shade to the resident fish population had been unmercifully cut back. The stark clay banks stared back at me, cracked and dry in the summer sun. They were as red and bare as a baboon's backside. The cover I had expected to find, so very essential to barbel location, was gone. In a matter of hours the axe and chainsaw had undone months of hard work and effort by Mick and me over the entire previous season, and totally jeopardized any thoughts we had that we would reap our just rewards for that endeavour.

What clown, I wondered, had made the ridiculous decision that a few small bushes and trees was hindering the progress of the Bristol Avon to the sea? As I walked the entire length, the scale of the devastation became all the more painfully obvious. Not a single vestige of cover had been left anywhere along the banks, and I knew that, without that cover, there would be nothing to hold the barbel in a shoal.

Our favourite swim looked basically the same in the water, with the bulk of the flow down the weed-free channel on the opposite bank, and the mid-river rush beds creating the normal pockets of slacker water behind them. Below the water line, therefore, the swim still had its same visual attraction, but the focal point of the area, the bush half-way along, under which the barbel had been resident, was conspicuous by its absence. The same bushes also held the flow back in the higher water levels of winter, thereby creating in their lee a steady current speed, ideal for the barbel to feed comfortably. Without the bushes, the current speed would surely be too fast.

Trying to make as light of my disappointment as possible, I baited the run and several of the rush-bed pockets in the normal manner, but to no avail. The evening and night were completely biteless. Not even a chub appeared to live in the area any longer.

I decided to move a fair way down river, to bait two more swims which had proved themselves to be reliable bite producers. On my arrival at this new area I was overwhelmed with a sense of frustrated anger.

Avon rapids.

Once more the butchers of the Wessex Water Authority had preceded me. Many tremendous swims, which had produced dozens of high-quality barbel the previous season, had received the treatment, and been wantonly destroyed. Willows had been scalped and all those lovely bankside bushes removed, so that there was no cover remaining. All fish life had departed, as had the prolific bird life that previously relied upon the riverside foliage for a livelihood. The birds had been forced to look for pastures new following this cruel rape of the environment.

I got to wondering how the river authorities continually get away with the destruction of the beauty of our river courses, and it made me feel even angrier when I realised that my rod licence fees help to pay the wages of the men who are at the forefront of this ruination of our waterways. Four months later, I came across the wrecking crew, still continuing their wanton destruction down to the sea, and despite a heated exchange, which at least released some of my pent-up aggression, I knew I was wasting my breath. While some desk-bound moron preaches conservation with one breath and then orders widespread devastation with the next, the natural beauty of our precious countryside will continue its sad decline.

I did not bother baiting any swims; after all, there was now no point in it. As I drove back to my first area my anger was turning into a deep depression. Once again I baited the clear channel and rush-bed pockets, as well as two other swims that had previously produced fish.

After a good meal in the van, and with the light intensity dropping fast, I crept back into position, determined to overcome the new handicap that had been placed in my way. It was, however, useless. Despite fishing very hard, rotating the swims in the manner which is so reliable, not the slightest indication of fish life did I see in over five hours of darkness. Reluctantly, I came to the inescapable conclusion that this section of river, which had produced dozens of big barbel before the bank clearance, was now totally devoid of fish. No longer was it the holding spot.

The drive home was a miserable affair. I knew that I would not be able to be on the river again until about November, and then Mick and I would have to start afresh in the location process.

During the winter of 1989–90 I fished the swim thirty or more times under varying conditions. The usual heavy baiting programme was undertaken at first, with no response whatever – not even a chub bite. However, I did take a barbel of 9lb 4oz, followed by an eight-pounder the next night, well upstream, and this new swim was baited hard after that, producing several more fish to over seven pounds during what remained of the winter. The original swim, however, where such heady success had been achieved a few short months before, remained completely unproductive – totally biteless.

The season was drawing to a close and, as usual, Tony and I had planned the last week in Hampshire. Either the Avon or the Stour would surely yield a nice fish as a finale to another campaign. With the van piled high with tackle, I set off for the Bristol Avon, which I intended to fish for a couple of days and nights before moving on to Hampshire to meet up with Tony.

The river was low and clear, but with a temperature of 48°F (9°C) I felt my chances of a few bites were quite good, and it would be nice to start off the week with a fish in the net. There was an ulterior motive also. For the last two years I had inexplicably blanked during the final four days of the season. At all costs, I wanted to avoid that particular hat trick.

During the first two hours of fishing I achieved my objective, with a chunky barbel of 5lb 3oz, a three-pounder and a fish of 7¼lb, which was instantly recognizable in that it had a pronounced kink in its back, and which I had first caught at the same weight over a mile upstream in November.

I then moved to the second baited swim, missing four bites in succession. Obviously, the fish in that particular shoal were badly spooked – not really surprising when you consider the attention that Mick and I had given them over the previous few weeks.

I awoke the next morning with the intention of driving to Hampshire, but over breakfast the four missed bites kept nagging at me. Eventually, I decided to stay one more night and go to join Tony the following day. The decision was to be justified, in that a slight modification in my bait presentation, in the swim where I had missed the bites, resulted in a securely hooked barbel of 9lb 7oz – an extremely pleasing capture. This was followed by another missed bite, and then a fish of 4lb 12oz concluded the session.

On impulse, I decided to fish the swim that had so far failed to yield a bite in over thirty attempts since the bank clearance operations, though this involved a drive in the dark of five miles upstream. Twenty minutes after my arrival I was tweaking my meat bait down that far-bank channel. The line twitched on my finger but no pull followed. I moved the bait, and then the line tightened decisively. At last an indication of a fish! To my annoyance, the bite was missed, but I was at least pleased that I had experienced a bite, after long months of fruitless effort. As I retrieved the terminal tackle to rebait, I noticed on the point of the hook a large barbel scale. Twenty minutes later I had packed up and was on my way to Hampshire. Now, though, I had hard evidence that barbel were once again in residence in the swim.

DOUBLE TOP

Matthew Bodily with a cracking eleven-pounder from the Great Ouse.

I arrived at the Mill Road car park by the Royalty fishery at Christchurch at about 1 a.m., with sleep my first priority. The week had started well and I was confident that tomorrow I would murder the barbel on the lower Royalty. As I pulled the sleeping bag over my head I began to laugh as I recalled an incident of two years before, at the same car park. I had been asleep for a short while when a knock on the side of the van made me wake with a start. I slid back the side door, fully expecting to see the boys in blue standing there, but all I found were two West Hampshire Water Board employees.

'We've been asked to give you this,' one said, handing me an envelope inscribed, 'To the owner of the white van'. Without another word, they turned and left.

Rubbing the sleep from my eyes, I wondered what this could possibly be about. Perhaps they wanted to name a swim after me, or offer me money to give barbel fishing lessons. I was already mentally negotiating my fee as I opened the envelope. It read: 'It has come to my attention

that you are sleeping in your van on West Hampshire Water Board property, and I must ask you to refrain from this practice. If you continue to do so we will take further action to stop this practice.'

I was dumbfounded. I could not believe what I had just read. It occurred to me that the author of the letter must really be on the ball. I had, after all, only been sleeping in the car park regularly for the past twenty years. Perhaps he was waiting to see whether a pattern was etablished.

The next morning the Avon was brimfull and really hammering down, though with not a trace of colour. It was going to be difficult, but with a water temperature of 49°F (10°C) conditions looked quite reasonable. An hour in the Telegraphs swim failed to meet with any response, and shortly afterwards I managed to miss my first bite from below the bypass bridge. After the swim had been rested for a while, another bait was again rolled down the gravel and this time there were no mistakes when the line tightened. After a terrific scrap, so typical of a Royalty barbel, I was looking at an immaculate fish of 7lb 10oz. I was well pleased.

In mid-afternoon the lead again moved, followed by a savage wrench on the rod top, and I was again connected to a powerful fish, which had intercepted the meat as it bounced down the heavy flow. The sun was shining and it was a lovely day, made perfect when the scales registered 8lb 2oz – my hundredth barbel of the season.

The session ended with a succession of missed bites which were little more than fast jabs. Royalty barbel have every right to be spooky. More than any other barbel in the country, they surely have seen it all.

I met up with Tony at the prearranged sleeping place and over several cups of tea we discussed the events of the start of our week's holiday. Tony had cracked a terrific chub of 5lb 7oz off a new stretch of the Stour, so, all in all, our week had got off to an encouraging start.

I decided I would fish the famous Throop fisheries on the Stour the following day, in the company of a great old friend of ours, Alf Tapley of Swindon, who used to live in Dorset. Alf was also down for a final week's holiday and had already met up with Tony on the Stour. His holiday had really started with a bang, as he had taken four four-pound-plus chub and one of 5lb 14oz in his first serious session.

After breakfast, as Tony favoured the upper Stour again, Alf and I embarked on a nostalgic trip together back to Throop, where, in the grand old days of Ernie Leah, we both used to be honorary bailiffs. Nostalgia, unfortunately, was all we did enjoy. It was the end of the season on a very popular fishery and there were far too many anglers about for successful barbel angling. Our only consolation in a very hard but enjoyable few hours was a solitary small chub.

After rejoining Tony for a meal in the evening I discovered that he had found the upper Stour hard going as well. The river was dropping fast and losing what little colour it had. All the signs pointed to fishing the feeder, and Tony decided to fish the river at Longham the next day, aiming to secure a swim where he had taken a large catch of barbel on the same method two years before. Alf fancied the Stour as well, but I had a feeling for the Royalty once again. It proved unfounded, however, and by mid-afternoon I was still biteless and wondering whether I should have elected to fish the feeder on the Stour with Tony. At 3 p.m., I packed up and drove the few miles to Longham to see how he was faring. In truth, the fishing there was equally grim. He had managed a solitary three-pound barbel, plus one of a similar size that had fallen off at the net, as well as being scared out of a year's growth when a cormorant took a small fish off his hook and flew out of the water straight at him.

A few hours after dark on a free stretch of the Stour also failed to produce a single barbel bite, and we were now getting very negative vibes about our barbel prospects in Hampshire. We have learned never to ignore such feelings, and Tony soon decided to head back to the Cherwell for the last few days. I plumped for the return journey to the Bristol Avon. That large barbel scale on the hook point was still fresh in my mind.

At 2 a.m., I was dropping hemp and corn, via the bait dropper, in the clear channel that had produced just the scale for me in countless hours of fishing since the previous winter. It occurred to me that I must be mad. I allowed the swim to settle over a cup of tea back at the van, and then returned to it full of determination.

Just after the first cast I felt a slight nudge on the line and then a pull, but my strike again met with thin air. On the hook was another barbel scale. Did I have to catch the fish bit by bit and then piece it together again to be able to weigh it? It was infuriating. After another twenty minutes of fruitless searching I turned it in for the night. After the long day, and the long drive back from Hampshire, I was badly in need of rest. I was not to emerge from my van until 2.30 the following afternoon. That's what I call a sleep!

I expected Mick Nicholls to come down for the last few days of the season, and, sure enough, his timing was as impeccable as usual, and he pulled into the car park beside me just as my kettle was coming to the boil. Over cups of tea I filled him in with the events of the week so far, and then we walked the banks, baiting a selection of swims in a section known to hold a good head of fish. With the temperature still at

48°F we both fancied our chances for a bite or two in the evening and night sessions to come.

That night we had several bites between us, Mick taking first prize with a cracking barbel of 10lb 2oz. What a superb start to his final session of the season! I managed two fish of 4¾lb and 5lb respectively, plus missing two good bites in the swim where I had caught the nine-pounder at the beginning of the week. It was three in the morning when we finally rolled into our sleeping bags, two exhausted but thoroughly contented barbel anglers.

The 'barbel scale swim' had been rested a full day and night, and I was racked with indecision as to whether to fish it the coming night or rest it a further twenty-four hours. After that, I would bait it heavily and put all my eggs in the one basket until the seaons's close.

At the crack of 11 a.m. the next day Mick and I were tucking into our calorie-controlled breakfast of bacon, sausages, egss, beans, tomatoes, mushrooms and toast – all washed down with half a gallon of tea – as we discussed our plans for another day's searching for that elusive Bristol Avon monster. Mick had decided to stick with the section he had taken the double from the previous night, while I eventually decided once again to rest the 'barbel scale swim' and investigate a down-river length which has proved very slow but certainly has the potential to turn up the barbel that dreams are made of.

My results during the hours of daylight were about par for the course, with only two small chub rewarding my efforts, but after dark, in my third baited swim, the proceedings began to liven up. I was fishing under a small far-bank bush and, tossing a piece of meat upstream, I slowly began to work it back down the glide. As the bait reached the bush where the bulk of the hemp was concentrated there was a pull.

A 10lb 2oz Bristol Avon fish is returned.

The firm strike connected with solid resistance, and I do mean solid. Whatever I had hooked was totally immovable at first. Gradually, by dint of pressure from several different directions, with as much force as the tackle would stand, the snag began to move. Slowly I was able to draw across the flow what appeared to be a large log festooned with weed and other debris. Beaching the mass in the margin, I began to sort it out when I felt a movement under the pile of rubbish. Thinking that I would discover a two-pound chub under there somewhere, I pulled away the rest of the weed. When I had uncovered the fish, I found to my surprise that it was a lovely mirror carp of about three pounds, and I quickly slipped my net back under it, allowing the snag to drift back down the river.

When I could not find my hook in the carp's mouth, I was starting to wonder what on earth was going on. There was a sudden vicious lunge on the rod and the clutch screamed. In seconds, thirty yards of line was stripped off the reel. Twenty thrilling minutes later I was to land the 'log', which had now been transformed into one very big and very angry pike, which thrashed the water to a foam as I lifted it out.

As I hauled it clear of the net mesh it was still fighting mad. It had probably been stalking the carp for hours when my piece of meat had arrived on the scene to completely wreck his supper. Obviously, what had happened was that the carp had intercepted the meat and had then been grabbed by the pike. Somehow or other, the hookhold had been transferred from the carp to the pike, both fish having become draped in weed and debris in the process. The pike's displeasure was still very evident during the weighing ceremony, as it continued its thrashing in the sling, but eventually it settled and the scales registered an impressive 23lb 6oz. After that, I eased the ugly brute back into the river and thanked her for half an hour's exciting action.

After that episode there was to be no further action, and I drove back up river to see how Mick was faring, finding him back in the swim in which he had landed the ten-pounder the night before. Tonight, however, there had been no such excitement; only two small chub had succumbed to his wiles. We had a good laugh as I recounted the saga of the carp and the pike, and then two tired anglers once again made their way back to the car park for a well earned and much needed rest.

The next day Mick again decided to stay on the baited swims, but I decided to travel back upstream and feed half a gallon of hemp and corn into the 'barbel scale' channel. After two days and nights of peace, I was quite confident that the barbel I had pricked, if still there, would be responsive to a hookbait. With luck, losing two of his outer garments would not have worried him unduly.

The day seemed to drag, with a couple of worm-caught chub the only action. I purposely left the baited channel alone all day, my intention being to search every inch of it after dark. If there was a barbel there, I'd have it.

An hour after dark I crept into position. My sense of anticipation was at fever pitch. A meat-paste bait plopped in a foot from the far bank, fifteen yards upstream of my position. The lead hit bottom, bounced once, and then held station in the steady flow. A tweak from me drew it a foot downstream, and then a lift and pull induced it to travel a yard further. I could clearly feel the gravel bottom as the lead and bait searched their way down it.

It held just upstream of my position, and then suddenly the line twitched in my left hand and then fell slack – a classic and umistakable bite. So unaware is the

Returning a muscular nine-pounder.

fish of danger when giving a bite to an upstream presentation that it is almost criminal to strike. But strike I did, and this time I connected with considerably more than a scale. The rod hammered over and I knew from the way that the fish did not move, but just held its position in the flow, that it was an extra-big barbel I had hooked.

I played that fish very firmly, allowing it to win only a few yards of line during the entire scrap. For ages it stayed deep and thumped the rod in an effort to dislodge my hookhold, but to no avail. I had strong tackle, and before long the fish rolled into the net at the first attempt. I knew it was a double, and was overcome by that feeling of elation only known to big-fish anglers. It is

a mixture of relief, satisfaction and sheer, almost uncontrollable excitement. If you talk to non-anglers about those emotions and the buzz you get from angling generally, all you get is a bemused blank expression. Yes, non-anglers are mighty strange people.

The scales confirmed 10lb 12oz of perfect barbel, and careful examination of the fish proved that it was the same fish of the previous season, when it had weighed 2oz less. My faith in the swim had at long last been justified. After placing the barbel in a sack, for Mick to take a photograph for me the following morning, I sat back to take it all in. After all the previous blanks, success had come at last. My season was going to finish on a high note. I cast back in

Lovely barbel at 10lb 12oz and 10lb 4oz – what a superb brace.

more the rod bent round to its fighting arc as another powerful adversary bore irresistibly upstream. Five minutes later the forceps were removing the size 4 Au Lion D'Or from my second double-figure barbel of the season. Ten pounds four ounces this one scaled. After all the months of nothing from the swim, I had taken two doubles in successive casts. Soon a second sack was in position, ready for Mick to record with his camera the results of an incredible night's barbel fishing.

Unbelievably, a third cast was to lead to a third tremendous barbel being hooked and for a long while I had visions of a hat-trick of doubles. It was not to be, however, and a fish of 8lb 3oz finally put the seal on an unforgettable night.

The next morning Mick duly obliged in the photographic department and, that task completed, the barbel were released together after we had ensured that they were able to cope with the current. We watched them disappear into midstream, wondering if we would make their acquaintance again.

After the disappointment of seeing the swim apparently ruined at the start of the season and the countless hours of unrewarded effort, it had finally come up trumps at the eleventh hour. Two double-figure barbel in two casts had been the thrilling climax of a week's fishing holiday that had proved to be, to put it mildly, extremely eventful.

again, and once more the meat began its steady progress down the gravel run, the line clearly visible in the bright moonlight. Again it twitched and fell slack and once

15 Barbel River Round-Up

This chapter provides a general appraisal of the present state of barbel rivers in this country and our thoughts on the future potential for big barbel in each of them. Where we have little or no personal experience of the fishing – on the Yorkshire rivers and the Hertfordshire Lea, for example – we have drawn on information gleaned from fellow members of the Barbel Catchers Club. Because of this, and to protect both our own fishing and that of our many barbel-fishing friends, you will find no information about accurate locations of big-barbel swims. That would be a betrayal of trust. We are only too happy to point you in the right direction, but you will have to do the specific investigative work yourselves.

THE DORSET STOUR

Without a doubt, some of the largest barbel in the country are resident in this most beautiful of barbel rivers, and some tremendous fish have been taken from its clear waters in recent seasons. It does not, however, give up its secrets easily, and it is a mistake to think that you only have to make the occasional trip to the Stour to be guaranteed a double. Like big barbel everywhere, they require much time and effort in tracking down, but if you are prepared to make that commitment the

rewards can make it very worthwhile indeed. Among the handful of rivers that we believe capable of throwing up a fish to substantially improve on the present barbel record, the Stour definitely comes high on the list.

Although there are certainly barbel as far upstream as Sturminster Newton, they are very few and far between, in small isolated groups, as far down as Longham bridge. In those many miles of river, location is the entire key to success, and with long stretches too deep for visual spotting of the fish it is a daunting prospect.

From Longham bridge downstream to the tidal river at Christchurch the barbel population shows a dramatic increase, and a great many barbel, including plenty of exceptionally big ones, are taken every season. The two local clubs that control the bulk of the fishing in this area are Ringwood and Christchurch, and we can offer no better advice than to say that if you only fished their waters you would have the opportunity of catching some of the biggest barbel in this country. You must, however, obey the rules imposed, as you should respect all angling club regulations. The two clubs mentioned do not allow night fishing, and you should expect to be severely dealt with if you are caught infringing that particular rule. Many of the stretches involved are controlled by wealthy landowners, and there is the ever-attendant risk that misbehaviour by a few thoughtless anglers

The Dorset Stour below Iford bridge.

could lose the fishing for everybody. The same comment applies to rod licences. Make sure that you purchase the appropriate document before you start fishing. The river authority bailiffs are on the ball in Hampshire and Dorset, and rightly so, and you can expect short shrift if you are caught without your licence. You have been warned.

The most famous Stour fishery is, of course, Throop, which is situated immediately downstream of Parley Green. Throop contains probably the greatest concentration of barbel in the river and it is therefore extremely popular. It is an excellent venue for the occasional visitor to the river, as you can reasonably expect to catch barbel on most days, although it is not as easy as press reports might sometimes indicate. As far as the potential for big fish is concerned, Throop certainly produces its crop of doubles each year, but we feel that the chances of an exceptional barbel – one to challenge the record – are poor, though certainly not impossible. Nevertheless, Throop cannot be recommended highly enough if you want excellent barbel fishing at a well run fishery with a good chance of a double-figure fish. We have spent many happy hours on its banks and still make the occasional trip back there for the sake of nostalgia. Barbel Corner, Pig Island, The Nettlebeds, Oak Tree Pool and other famous swims have given countless anglers many hours of pleasure. If you have not as yet fished Throop, give it a try. A Dorset Stour barbel could be your reward.

THE HAMPSHIRE AVON

The Hampshire Avon and barbel are synonymous, and certainly the river's reputation as the premier barbel fishery in the country is well deserved. Undoubtedly, there are some mammoth fish in the Avon which have not as yet picked up an angler's

bait and, although we hesitate to speculate on the top weight possible, we certainly feel that there is a very real chance of a fish turning up in the 15–16lb class.

As with the Dorset Stour, the further up river you go the more and more localized the barbel shoals become, and the lower the overall population. The compensation is, however, that some of the individual barbel in the middle river are undoubtedly huge, and a dedicated campaign could yield exciting results. Like the Stour, however, the problem of location could well prove heart-breaking and you need to have the right mental approach to be able to cope with the countless blanks that such a campaign would surely involve.

While barbel are certainly present above

A streamlined six-pounder from the Severals fishery on the Avon.

Salisbury, it is really only from Salisbury downstream that they are of particular interest to us as anglers. Areas such as Britford, Downton and Fordingbridge are better known for the superb quality of their general coarse fishing, but they do produce a handful of exceptional barbel each season. Certainly, the chances of a twelve-pound fish are high, but the tempo of the barbel fishing is very slow. There is not the head of fish for it to be otherwise.

One of the better-known areas combining a reasonable head of barbel with the chance of an outsize specimen is Ibsley, which produced a fully authenticated sixteen-pounder to a salmon angler many years ago. Downstream of Ibsley, the population of barbel starts to increase progressively, and when we reach Ringwood, and the famous Severals fisheries, the prospects become good even for the casual visitor. Because of the large head of barbel on the Severals, the average size of the fish suffers somewhat, but the fishery still produces a good crop of doubles each season, with at least one fish approaching or just over twelve pounds reported. At this time, we feel it extremely unlikely that the Severals is capable of producing a barbel to challenge the current record. As is the case with the Stour, the sparsely populated upper stretches are more likely to harbour such an individual.

Moving on down to Christchurch, we pass Winkton, itself a tremendously productive big-barbel area which is well worth more than an occasional visit, before arriving at the famous Royalty fishery, which every angler in the country must surely have heard of. On the Royalty – which is really a river within a river, as the barbel population there has been so intensely pursued as to have formed its own behaviour pattern – the barbel is the predominant species, and the average size of the fish lower than almost anywhere else on the

Avon. Under the right conditions large catches of barbel are possible from this very popular fishery and, like Throop, it cannot be recommended highly enough for the sheer pleasure of barbel fishing. You must not, however, expect to break any records there. We do not believe that any really exceptional barbel are now present in the Royalty, with the possible exception of one individual fish which has occasionally been observed in the Parlour. Most of the double-figure fish reported from the Royalty each season amount to just two or three individual barbel continually being recaptured. That is an absolutely confirmed fact. There is nothing whatever wrong with a recapture, of course, but if you are striving to beat a personal best it is as well to know the potential of the water in which you are concentrating your efforts. If a true leviathan barbel is your target, then the Royalty is not the place where that ambition will be realized – not at the moment, anyway. Nonetheless, the Royalty has produced many monstrous barbel in the past and we hope it will do so in the future.

A unique folklore has built up around the Royalty, and its swims are famous the length and breadth of the country. The upper river, that section upstream of the footbridge at the main car park, is not available for coarse fishing after the end of January because of the onset of the salmon season. At the top of the fishery is the Great Weir, home of many of the Royalty's barbel. If it is an eight-pounder you are after, the Great Weir would be a sound bet. On the left-hand bank (looking downstream) the bank is available to normal permit holders, and one of the top-rate swims is towards the tail end of the pool, roughly adjacent to the upstream extremity of the small central island. Legering upstream in mid-pool, we have both taken dozens of good fish from this swim, and it is highly recommended. The right-hand bank is

The footbridge across the famous Royalty.

called the Compound, and must be booked in advance. We have never fished it, but large catches have been recorded from here. You pay your money and take your choice.

Downstream on the left-hand bank the opportunity to see the quarry presents itself in the upper and lower Trammels. Hot spots in this section vary from day to day as the shoals move around, a direct result of angling pressure. The run below the bottom salmon angler's hut is probably as consistent as any. Our favourite swim on the Royalty is the short length from the

entrance to the little weir down to Engineers point, a brilliantly consistent swim. Dozens of large barbel have picked up our baits here. A few more yards downstream and we arrive opposite the second stream confluence, which is the outflow from the famous Parlour. Like the Compound, the Parlour is available for fishing only by booking, and it is not cheap. Results, however, can be spectacular.

Below the confluence with the Parlour outlet, day-ticket anglers have access to both banks and many famous swims are found in close proximity. On the left bank

160

below the two pipes that cross the river and above the railway bridge are Harrigans and the Railway Pool, while on the right bank are Engineers (the trees just above the pipes), the Pipe Slack, Greenbanks and the lower Railway Pool. Below the railway bridge on both banks is known as Fiddler's, leading into the Piles swim on the left bank and the Boathouse swim on the right. Directly in front of the main fishery office is located a lovely swim known as the Housepool. Any one of these swims and all areas between are capable of providing a memorable day's barbel fishing. Top choice for bites would be Greenbanks, summer or winter. The Pipe and Harrigans are also very consistent, the Pipe particularly offering a high average of seven-

pound-plus fish. Either side of the Railway can be slow at times but a double could be the reward of patience and determination. Fiddler's, again a consistent bite producer throughout the season, is particularly prolific on the left bank, being stacked with fish in flood conditions. The Piles and Boathouse are slower bite-wise, but the fish are of a higher average size, with an elusive double being on the cards, particularly in the Boathouse.

The lower Royalty water commences below the footbridge and is open all season for coarse fishing. Although it is less densely stocked with barbel, there are several swims which are as consistent as any on the upper river. The Housepool has a resident group, and nine-pound barbel appear in

A cracking Avon double.

catches of six or more fish in a day. The Pylons and Telegraphs will also produce the goods, summer or winter. Below the bypass, on both banks, although heavily weeded in the summer months, eight-pound-plus fish are landed each season. Johnson's and the Waterloo Stream, right and left respectively, are the bottom boundaries of the Royalty fishery, with Johnson's the right-hand fork, the better of the two in our experience.

Every named swim on the Royalty – and others that have no name – has produced its share of barbel over the years, and, as at Throop, we have a wealth of treasured memories of many thousands of contented hours spent on the banks of this most famous of fisheries. One myth that we would like to dispel is that Royalty barbel are easy. They are not. In fact, special techniques have to be learned to regularly catch them. Of all barbel, Royalty fish are the most educated. Correct bait presentation is of the essence. The Royalty is a superb fishery. We love the place.

The Royalty fisheries apart, the Ringwood and Christchurch clubs control large sections of the Avon, for very reasonable annual subscriptions in view of the superb quality of the fishing, but quite a few miles of the river are also available to day-ticket anglers, some of it also being available at night. As well as at the Royalty, there are certainly day-ticket facilities at Winkton, Bisterne, Ringwood, Fordingbridge and Breamore, as well as many other venues,

Bob James fishes below a Hampshire Avon weir.

162

and your best bet is to contact one of the local tackle shops to acquaint yourself with up-to-date information on water avail-ablity. One of the best shops to contact is undoubtedly Davis of Christchurch, where Royalty permits are obtained. All information on the fishing in Hampshire and Dorset is freely given by the owner, Graham Pepler, himself an extremely competent all-round angler, and many of the day-tickets necessary are sold by Graham.

THE SEVERN AND ITS TRIBUTARIES

In recent years, the Severn has produced some monstrous barbel, topped by Howard Maddocks's record of 16lb 3oz and Dave Jenkins's monster of 15lb 15oz, from the lower river in full spate. As well as these colossal fish, the river has produced countless doubles, with several topping 14lb, and the potential is exciting indeed. The number of doubles is quite mind-blowing, there being shoals of fish of this size. Trefor can relate one instance of four bites yielding three ten-pounders plus a 12lb 15oz, and catches of two or more doubles in a session are commonplace. Nor are these giant fish confined to small localized areas. Doubles have been reported from as high upstream as Atcham down to below Tewkesbury, which is a lot of river. The problem, of course, is the old one of location. While there are many areas of shallows where spotting is possible in the summer, there are also many long stretches where the water is too deep. Over several years, groups of dedicated barbel special-ists have been giving comparatively short sections of the river a very thorough searching, and even now they are only just beginning to achieve any kind of con-sistency in their catches. The Severn is a

wide, deep and powerful river, and any man who regularly catches big barbel from it thoroughly deserves to.

The furthest upstream we have personal experience of is at Atcham, where there is a well-known free stretch, available to anyone who has purchased a Severn-Trent rod licence. A terrific head of good barbel inhabits the river here, and one of the most famous swims is the well-known Snag swim, only a few yards from the car park at the top boundary. The snag is actually a sunken wall, now completely clothed in thousands of yards of line, and many big fish have been landed and lost from this swim. A great many years ago, when a seven-pounder was a big fish from the Severn, our old mate Merv Wilkinson took a fabulous fish of 9lb 6oz from that swim. If you want to catch your first Severn barbel you can do no better than start at Atcham.

Moving downstream, the next well-known venue we come to is Ironbridge, where there is again a good head of barbel, and plenty of big ones. This is one of the areas reputed to hold monsters, even fish of record proportions, and it will be in-teresting to watch developments over the next few seasons.

The head of barbel remains good through Bridgnorth, Hampton Loade and Stourport, but it is below the confluence with the Teme, where the lower Severn can be considered to start, that big-barbel specialists have been concentrating their attention in recent years. The river between Worcester and Upton-on-Severn has produced a great many fish well into double figures in a comparatively short time, and, as many of these have been well over twelve pounds, the prospects are very exciting indeed.

The Severn can be a heart-breaking river to fish. As well as its sheer physical size and depth, there is the ever-attendant possibility of conditions deteriorating so rapidly as to kill the prospects for catching barbel stone dead. This can occur summer and winter, unfortunately. In low water conditions, the level-regulating dam at Llyn Clywedog releases what is known as compensation water into the river, which is both very cold and almost totally de-oxygenated. The effect this has on sport is dramatic. The negative effects of very rapid drops in water temperature on barbel behaviour have been described in Chapter 5. On no river are such rapid drops more prevalent than on the Severn, as a result of the compensation policy.

Conversely, in unsettled weather, what is only average rainfall in the Midlands can be a heavy and sustained downpour lasting several days in the Welsh moutains, where the Severn has its source. Several inches of rain in a day is very common, and this leads to extremely rapid rises in level. Two feet in an hour has been recorded, and that is an incredible volume of water. Also, as the water has it source in the mountains, the floodwater is usually very cold, producing further detrimental effects. At its most extreme, the water can consist entirely of melted snow, which may not be obvious if you are fishing the middle river on a mild day. The thermometer is an essential tool if you are serious about fishing the Severn for barbel.

One more important point relative to the speed with which the river can come up into spate, which will sometimes see it as much as fifteen feet above normal level, is the consideration of safety. In many places the banks are extremely steep and very slippery, and no attempt should be made to start fishing until you are happy that you can get back up the bank in a hurry if you have to. It is not too dramatic to say that there are some areas where we would advise taking strong pegs and a rope ladder, just as a precaution. The Severn must be treated with respect.

A multitude of clubs control the fishing on the Severn, and any local tackle shop will advise on permits. One club which controls more than most is Birmingham Anglers Association, and if you acquire their book a great many miles of superb fishing will be available to you.

The important tributaries of the Severn are the Teme and the Warwickshire Avon, together with its feeder the Warwickshire Stour. The Teme boasts large shoals of barbel and although of low average size, increasing numbers of double figure fish are showing, to over 13lb. Without a doubt, the Teme could throw up an unexpected surprise. The same comments apply to the Warwickshire Stour, where big fish have certainly been seen but where the average capture at the moment is around 4lb.

The Warwickshire Avon could be the river of the future. When this book was first released, we said that the river would be the one to watch in years to come. Eight years on, and the Avon is producing large bags of barbel in many areas and plenty of double-figure fish. Not only that, but we know of at least one genuine 14lb fish plus unconfirmed reports of a 17lb fish electro-fished from the middle reaches. The growth rate of Avon barbel is exceptional and it is by no means inconceivable that a couple more seasons could see it rivalling the Severn and Great Ouse for the new record.

THE KENNET

The Kennet is truly a beautiful river, and we have both often said that it is one to which we should devote a lot more attention – it is such a pleasure to fish. The trouble is that we are always looking for that extra-big fish, and this is where the Kennet can be so frustrating. As it is one of the few waterways in the country where the barbel are truly indigenous, the head of fish is very large indeed, leading to excellent sport with average-sized barbel, but making the odds against catching an exceptional fish quite long. Very few doubles are reported from the Kennet each season, an eight-pounder being quite hard to come by in most sections.

As with every river, those areas where there seem to be fewer barbel are also most likely to produce the extra-large specimen; and, as with chub, those lengths where the river is deeper and steadier – untypical of the Kennet, if you like – are the best bet. Much of the river between Newbury and Thatcham is of this character, and indeed has produced many of the bigger fish reported from the Kennet over the years. It is

almost certain that the odd monster could inhabit the river above Newbury, possibly up as far as Hungerford, but there is no doubt that location would be a major headache. Access would also be difficult as much of this upper river is preserved for fly fishing, so barbel fishing upstream of Newbury is not really a realistic proposition.

The middle stretches of the river through Woolhampton and Aldermaston, where we have spent countless happy hours, are positively teeming with barbel, and here you will be hard pressed to catch a fish as big as eight pounds. Seven-pounders are not that common. Please do not think that we are being in any way derogatory. Nothing could be further from the truth. If you wish to enjoy your barbel

A nine-pounder is returned to a flooded Teme.

fishing, without being concerned about the size of the individual fish, we can recommend no river so highly as the Kennet.

Moving downstream towards the confluence with the Thames below Reading, we come first of all to the stretch at Burghfield before reaching Reading itself. In these lower sections the average size of the barbel again begins to rise, and there are plenty of seven- and eight-pound fish to be found. Double-figure fish are taken very occasionally from these stretches, but a Kennet double, even from here, is still a rarity. The famous Jam Factory stretch of the river at Reading is where a thirteen-pounder was reported about fifteen years ago, but that has to be seen as a freak fish for the river. Even in the less densely populated stretches of the Kennet, we feel that

the chances of a new record barbel are practically non-existent at the present time.

While several clubs control short sections of bank between Newbury and Reading, the club that gives access to the bulk of the river is Reading and District Angling Association. Unfortunately, it can be difficult to obtain this permit if you live outside the area, and also the club imposes a night-fishing ban on most stretches, which is strictly enforced. If you want to fish at night, when the chances of a bigger than average fish are certainly enhanced, then you can try the free town water at Newbury. Failing that, some of the smaller clubs and day-ticket fisheries allow night fishing, but you will have to make your own inquiries about those.

Marsh Pratley with an upper Thames specimen.

THE THAMES AND ITS TRIBUTARIES

Without a shadow of doubt, there are a tremendous number of big barbel in the River Thames, countless double-figure fish having been taken from nearly every section over the years. Certainly, it is one of those rivers where we have no hesitation in saying that a new record is always a possibility.

Perhaps more than with any other river, location of the fish on the Thames, along almost its entire length, is the major obstacle to consistent success with barbel. It is both wide and deep, as well as lacking the clarity of, say, the Kennet, and the fishing is more a case of locating features to fish at rather than finding the fish themselves. That great Thames barbel angler John Everard advocated fishing in the vicinity of cabbage patches or areas where the river narrows, and his results suggest that you could do a lot worse than follow that simple advice.

The average size of Thames barbel is very good, as good as anywhere in the country, and the river is well worth a concerted effort if you are looking for that elusive double or just regular confrontations with eight-pound-plus fish. There are so many good areas that it is almost impossible to give anything but very vague advice, but areas with a tremendous track record would include Lechlade, Radcot, Buscot, above and below Tadpole Bridge at Witney, Newbridge, Eynsham, Northmoor, Bablock Hythe, Wallingford, Abingdon and Pangbourne. Some of the biggest barbel ever produced by the Thames have come in and immediately around Oxford. The famous Medley stretch comes to mind, where very many double-figure fish have put in an appearance, including several over twelve pounds and a reputed thirteen-pounder.

Fishing the river around and in Oxford can, however, be an exercise in total frustration, especially in summer, as the boat traffic can make serious angling almost impossible at times. On the very popular Port Meadow fishery at Godstow it is not unusual to see one boat every ten minutes throughout the daylight hours in summer. The only possible barbel angling is at night or in the runs immediately below the weirs. These are usually free of boat traffic since the boats moving along the river cannot negotiate the weirs and have to divert through the lock cuttings. Luckily for Thames barbel anglers, most of the river is accessible for night fishing, and the best approach is to spend the daylight hours preparing the ground for an after-dark assault.

One of the better-known areas for very big barbel in the town itself is the stretch at Abbey Road, where it follows along a length of back gardens. For many years exceptional fish have been reported from this length of river, but it is extremely slow fishing, with obviously a very small head of barbel. An occasional bite is all you can reasonably expect. We have to say that the fishing at Abbey Road is not our cup of tea any more, although we fished it quite a lot a few years ago. This is not because of the difficulty of the fishing, which has never worried us, but because there are other distractions to contend with which certainly destroy the enjoyment of barbel angling. Anglers have been attacked along the towpath, by both drunks and glue sniffers, as well as having valuable tackle either stolen or thrown in the river, and instances of this kind of behaviour are unfortunately increasing. If a double-figure barbel is worth that kind of hassle, then you will certainly deserve any success that comes your way.

As well as the Thames itself, each of the

tributaries that flow into it in the Oxford area have, in their time, produced a few very big barbel, generally in the few miles immediately above the confluence with the main river. Huge barbel have been reported from the Windrush, the Evenlode, the Seacourt Stream and the Cherwell. From our own fishing, we have the best knowledge of the Cherwell, but the barbel fishing on all these tributaries follows a similar pattern, with fish being found dotted here and there in small groups which are not very easy to pin down. The location difficulties are, however, outweighed a little by the high average weight of the fish, and, if they can be found, an eight-pounder will not be too hard to come by. Be prepared, however, to put in a lot of work in finding the barbel. Our experience has shown that accurate location is essential, certainly on the Cherwell. Many experienced Cherwell anglers have never even seen a barbel in many years fishing. Only in the 1989–90 season were they caught with

any consistency, but that was only after more than five years of hard searching, during which time very few barbel indeed were caught. Even now, only four groups of fish have been located, so this kind of barbel fishing is by no means easy. If you have the right temperament, however, it is very rewarding.

For fishing in and around the Oxford area, the club to join is the Oxford Alliance, or one of the myriad clubs affiliated to it. Membership of this organization will give you enough barbel waters to fish for a lifetime. There are few restrictions, membership being open to all, and all the fishing tackle shops in Oxford itself will be able to provide the necessary documents. Do not forget your Thames River Authority rod licence. The bailiffs are on the ball, and you are assured of prosecution if you are caught fishing without the necessary authority. Again, you have been warned.

The lower Thames, from below Reading, currently seems to be in something of a

The head of a Cherwell twelve-pounder.

decline as far as large barbel are concerned. We do not fish it ourselves, but men who do report that the average fish is getting smaller. An interesting fact here is that lower Thames carp are increasing both in numbers and weight, thirty-pounders now being caught, though many of the captures are being kept very quiet. Possibly the two factors are related.

As with the Thames generally, the boat traffic on the lower river means that the serious barbel angler – and carp angler, come to that – is well advised to seek his quarry after dark, when he can be guaranteed a little peace.

Just as the tributaries that feed the Thames around Oxford contain a handful of bigger than average barbel, so do the lower river tributaries – in particular the Wey, the Mole and the Colne. The Colne especially has produced some colossal fish in recent seasons. Certainly, every tributary of the Thames is worthy of thorough investigation for big barbel.

THE GREAT OUSE

What an exciting river the Great Ouse is becoming once again, after years in the doldrums! The last few seasons have seen an impressive number of twelve-pound fish come to net, plus at least two definite thirteen-pounders. It is true to say that the Ouse is something of an enigma, for while barbel are indigenous to the river (as they are to the Kennet) it has never really been seriously fished for its barbel until comparatively recently.

However, the barbel have never exploded in numbers as they have in the Kennet, the Ouse being in the main a river of very different character, and that is why it offers exciting possibilities for the man seeking exceptionally big fish. Make no

mistake, there are barbel to be caught in the Great Ouse to rival the best that Hampshire has to offer, and we would not be at all surprised to see the next barbel record from the river. The Great Ouse is no different from all the other rivers discussed where the barbel are of a high average weight, in that the population density of the fish is low and unevenly spread. In exactly the same way as the Cherwell, for example, there seem to be long stretches where no barbel are to be found and others where two or three groups have taken up residence. Location of these groups of fish is obviously the first essential for a potentially successful campaign, and that is where the first difficulty is encountered. Long sections of the Ouse are simply too deep, even in summer, for visual location to be a proposition, and you have to resort to the time-consuming baiting and searching techniques discussed in Chapter 5. There are no short cuts; where there is little or no visual evidence to guide you, it is hard work, taking a great many blank sessions before barbel are located. You can, of course, watch the angling media for fish reports and stories of barbel being landed in matches. However, every other interested angler will be doing exactly the same thing, so we feel that it is far better to quietly find your own fish. Using press reports to give you a guide to general areas is certainly acceptable, as that will obviously save much valuable time, but do not be so narrow-minded as to find out which is the going swim and then simply occupy it until you have caught the same fish. That approach to catching big fish gives very little satisfaction and causes a lot of ill feeling.

Until quite recently almost all the big-barbel reports from the Ouse were concentrated round the middle reaches – say, from Bedford to St Ives. In the late seventies and early eighties, this general area turned up quite a few eleven- and twelve-pound fish, although the anglers concerned had to work tremendously hard, suffering innumerable blanks, for the success they had. There then followed quite a lean spell for a few years until about 1986, when the Ouse barbel started to come back strongly. The most exciting feature of this latest development is that the upper river is now producing a lot more barbel than it ever did before, and some of them are very big fish indeed. There have certainly been several twelve-pounders caught well upstream of Bedford in the last two seasons, and this is only one symptom of the recovery of the upper Ouse generally, which had been a pale shadow of its once glorious self. The superb quality of upper Ouse chub and roach, as well as barbel, and the rapid weight gain of all species, gives us great encouragement for the future.

It is impossible to define the upstream extremity of the spread of barbel, though they certainly are present as high as Stony Stratford. The coming seasons may see their migration in numbers higher still, but certainly at the moment a barbel campaign upstream of that area would be a daunting prospect.

Almost all the clubs that control the fishing on the great Ouse are easy of entry and reasonably priced, most of the river being also available for night fishing. We will not attempt to itemize the multitude of clubs involved; any of the tackle shops in Bedford or Northampton will be able to put you right on access to any stretch you fancy having a crack at.

THE WENSUM

Of all the barbel rivers discussed in this chapter, the Wensum is probably the most extensively researched, since the comparatively short length of river containing the bulk of the barbel is very heavily fished indeed. Nowhere is the potential for big fish known better than on the Wensum, where every double-figure fish is a recognized individual. That is why, despite the tremendous barbel the river has produced, and despite the thousands of happy hours we have both spent there, we feel it unlikely that the Wensum will in the foreseeable future produce a barbel to beat our old mate Dave Plummer's record of 13lb 6oz.

In assessing the potential of any river, we always work on a combination of logic and statistics, hence our stressing the importance of recognizing individual fish. It is a fact that every reported double-figure barbel taken from the Wensum in the last three years has been a recapture of a known fish – with only one exception, an eleven-pounder to Chris Shortis which had never been seen before. The result of this pressure is that most of the fish are losing weight. Obviously, the capture of one new fish suggests that other captures are possible. We did hear rumours of a new fish of 13lb 8oz but we were never able to confirm it as fact.

There is a further problem which does not augur well for the barbel-holding stretch of the Wensum, and that is that the new weir at Costessy allows access upstream for the fairly small head of barbel, thus making their future location much more of a lottery. Also, the well publicized new water extraction levels for the river mean that the flow is drastically reduced, to such an extent that in a dry summer, like that of 1989, the weir actually stops flowing. It does not take a genius to work out the result of a pollution coinciding with a river at ultra-low level. There would be a major catastrophe, and unfortunately we, along with many concerned Norfolk anglers, feel that this is a tragedy just waiting to happen. That is one reason why

Trefor with one of his many Wensum monsters.

committed men such as Chris Turnbull are doing such sterling work with the Norfolk Anglers' Consultative Association (NACA) – including the introduction, with full official blessing, of new barbel stocks into the river above the new abstraction point. The Wensum is obviously capable of producing a crop of very big, healthy barbel, and must at all costs be preserved as a barbel fishery for future generations of anglers.

Present access for barbel fishing on the Wensum is very poor, most of the known areas being syndicated. There is a free stretch of river at Green Lane near Norwich, which has produced the occasional fish, but that area is a far more reliable chub fishery. We must stress that under no circumstances should you attempt to fish any of the syndicated stretches without first having obtained the relevant permission. You will be asked to leave if you are caught poaching.

THE BRISTOL AVON

In just a few short years, the Bristol Avon has risen from relative obscurity to being one of the premier barbel rivers in the country. It has produced a remarkable number of double-figure fish in a very short time, as well as large numbers of barbel, which is in itself quite an unusual combination. Perhaps most exciting is the fact that very big fish are turning up from all stretches of the river, and the potential is therefore almost unlimited. It has already produced several eleven- and twelve-pounders, as well as dozens of ten-pounders, and the prospects for the future are quite mouth-watering. It is really astounding how, in just thirty-six years since their initial introduction, barbel have colonized the Avon quite so

BARBEL RIVER ROUND-UP

*Personal best from the Bristol Avon
– 12lb 10oz.*

extensively. The river is obviously ideally suited to them.

Availability of the fishing on the river is very good, with easy access to the clubs that control the bulk of the bank, the two best being Chippenham AA and Bristol Amalgamated. Membership of these two organizations allows you to fish many areas, from as high up river as Malmesbury right down to the tidal reaches around Keynsham, just upstream of Bristol itself. In truth, the barbel are found in isolated pockets only as high up river as Malmesbury, and it is at about Chippenham that the barbel becomes a really prolific Avon species. As with many other rivers we have discussed, however, the upper reaches could well harbour one or two monsters,

which would require a lot of time and dedication to track down. Above Malmesbury access becomes more difficult and, although there would undoubtedly be the odd barbel to be found, much of the river is reserved for trout interests and therefore out of bounds to barbel anglers.

It is difficult to say whether the river is capable of producing a record-shaking specimen. There is a very big difference between twelve-pound barbel and fish of over fourteen pounds. The rate at which the fish are growing suggests that the possibilities of a new record in the next few years are very real, but we feel it very likely that the bigger fish might soon peak in weight, or may already have done so, in much the same way as the larger Wensum barbel seem to be maintaining or losing weight. Many of the better-known areas, where a large number of the double-figure fish have been caught, are now quite heavily fished, with the result that the barbel are coming under increasing pressure. This is never conducive to achieving maximum weight. The saving grace, however, is that the Avon is a big river, with many miles of still largely neglected water. It is from one of these latter areas that a monster fish could soon put in an appearance.

One important point about the Bristol Avon is that it is a river of very dangerous high banks in places, and raging floodwater can raise the level by many feet in a remarkably short space of time. In this it is very much like the Severn. Please treat the river with respect, taking care to watch your footing. There are sections that we fish where it would be extremely difficult to climb out should you fall in, especially if there were higher and faster water than normal. With that in mind, a landing net with a long extendible handle is an article of equipment that is essential on much of this river.

'Ace' Nicholls with a beautiful 10lb 2oz Bristol Avon fish.

THE LEA

One river of which we have no first-hand experience whatever is the Hertfordshire Lea, and all the comments that follow are from information supplied from fellow members of the Barbel Catchers Club.

Although there are isolated pockets of fish in the river above Hertford, it is below that town that the river becomes worth fishing for barbel at the moment. This could, however, change in the near future, as the Thames Water Authority has recently introduced new stock to the upper reaches of the river.

On the Lea it is the weirs and the lengths immediately downstream of them that have the best barbel pedigree, and two of the best, as well as being the most popular, are the Crown Fishery Carthagena Weir at Broxbourne, and the very well known King's Weir at Wormley. The latter fishery supports a very large head of barbel, but they are pursued intensely throughout the season, and for that reason an exceptionally big barbel is extremely unlikely.

Access to the fishing on the Lea is very mixed. On the Crown Fishery, although tickets are issued for the weir, there is a very long waiting list. The fact that the weir supports a head of very large carp to over twenty pounds is no help, as the carp anglers have reason to prize the permits as much as do barbel anglers. In King's Weir

The famous Kennet fishery Aldermaston Mill.

itself only six anglers are permitted to fish at any one time, three on each side, and, as will be appreciated, those pegs are always much in demand. However, access to the river downstream of the weir is quite good, with just over a mile controlled by Redland Angling, which anyone can join. Apparently there are about seventy swims on that length of river, many of them having produced fish into double figures.

THE YORKSHIRE RIVERS

It has to be said right from the outset that if we know nothing about the Lea we know even less about the rivers of Yorkshire, and so once again we have been heavily reliant on our friends in the Barbel Catchers Club.

The most obvious comment about the fishing in Yorkshire is that you must lower your sights if you are to enjoy your pursuit of barbel, since a seven-pounder has to be rated a specimen. Because of generally much lower average water temperatures and lower fertility than in the more southerly rivers, and the fact that the Yorkshire Ouse system is given to frequent high spate flooding (because, with the exception of the Derwent the rivers drain the Pennines), the barbel never enjoy the same undisturbed feeding conditions as they do in more favourable environments. For this reason, the capture of a double-figure fish from Yorkshire is an exceedingly rare event.

The rivers of interest to the barbel angler are the Yorkshire Ouse itself and its tributaries the Wharfe, the Swale, the Ure, the

174

Nidd and the Derwent. As is usually the case, the tributaries are often a better bet for the man seeking a specimen barbel, and certainly over recent seasons the average size of fish from the Swale and the Derwent would suggest they are favourite for an outsize specimen. On the Derwent in particular, the average size of the barbel is quite exceptional for the north of England but, as you would expect, they are very few and far between. Good average size is almost always associated with a low stock density.

The best barbel we know of from Yorkshire is a specimen of 12lb 6oz from the Derwent, a truly immense fish from that county. Despite that superb capture, we have to say that the chances of a barbel to challenge the present record from that part of the world are almost non-existent.

THE WYE

In the 1990s, the Wye and its tributary the Lugg have exploded on the barbel scene in a big way, and some exceptional fish have been taken from the Wye in recent seasons. As yet, nothing has been reported to the press to challenge the Severn, Ouse or Wensum monsters, but it is surely only a matter of time. Much of the Wye is still of unknown potential, although the stretches at Bredwardine and Belmont Lodge are now well known, largely due to the efforts of our old friend John Bailey.

The Wye offers barbel angling a very exciting future, but it is a big river and the fishing is by no means easy. As always, location is of the essence, but the rewards are there for anglers with perseverance. At the moment, the river is wide open to those with a pioneering spirit, because there are undoubtedly as yet undiscovered monsters to catch.

THE TRENT

The trend for a cleaner Trent catchment area in recent years has seen ever more exciting results with big barbel, with certainly an increase in the average size of the fish and several sections now containing barbel of a size to rival those of the Ouse and the Severn. This is particularly true of the Trent weirpools, where some huge fish abound to compete with the large carp and chub.

Also exciting now is the Dove, a lovely weed-filled, sparkling stream, where reports of large barbel seen and lost are becoming too common to ignore.

At the time of writing (November 1998) the barbel record situation is changing with bewildering speed. So far this season, Howard Maddocks's 16lb 3oz Severn fish has been beaten no fewer than three times by the same Wensum fish, at a maximum weight of 16lb 13oz, as well as being equalled and then beaten by the same fish on the Ouse. Particularly interesting to Tony is the fact that the Ouse barbel, caught in late October at 16lb 12oz is the same fish that he took in July 1997 at 14lb 2oz, an astonishing weight gain. We await the outcome of the deliberations of the Record Fish committee on the 16lb 13oz Wensum barbel, while being confident that this coming winter will see the first ever 17lb fish falling to rod and line.

16 Hurricane Barbel

Trefor West

Heavy rain had persisted for the best part of a week, not localized to the south or west coasts but blanketing the entire country with an incessant downpour from thick black clouds. The television weather men had said that they saw no immediate end to the wet conditions, and hinted vaguely that things could get a lot worse before they got better. When they predicted that wind

Our first ever double is returned to the Wensum – it weighed in at 12lb 12oz.

speed could increase possibly to severe gale force, events proved them to be masters of the understatement.

Unperturbed by the conditions, I headed for Norfolk, and more particularly the barbel of the River Wensum. The river had been carrying extra water for two or three days and, as an influx of fresh water is often the signal for barbel to go on a mad feeding spree, the fishing can often be brilliant, if the timing of a trip is such as to coincide with the extra water peaking in level and beginning to fine off. I was excited about the trip; little did I realize what lay in store for me over the next seven days and nights.

From my home town of Coventry to any of the better barbel venues involves a substantial amount of travelling, but most of the journeys are quite fast and pleasant. Unfortunately, that cannot be said about the A47 trunk road to Norwich, which is nothing more than a tedious drag. The endless procession of heavy lorries, belching out their polluting diesel fumes makes for frustratingly slow progress, and it is always with a great sense of relief that I eventually turn off for Costessy.

The river was bank-high and coloured, as I expected, and when the thermometer recorded a temperature of 46°F (8°C) I realized that things were looking good. The rain had eased a little as I began my pre-baiting operations; I was soon to discover that that was the lull before the storm –

176

literally. A gallon and a half of mixed corn and hemp was deposited in three swims, in the areas where bites had been experienced in previous seasons under similar water conditions. With the point swim, the copse and the bottom bend primed for action, it was time to retire to the van for an afternoon snooze.

I woke to the sound of lashing rain on the side of the van, and after a good meal and three mugs of tea there was no sign of the rain abating so I put the kettle on again. I remember thinking that, with seven days in front of me, there was no reason to venture out in those foul weather conditions. It would ease off shortly, I thought. It did not, and, with no sign of it doing so, I realized that old Westy faced a wet Wednesday night on the Wensum. Great fun, this barbel fishing, isn't it?

All the gear went on – thermal suit, waders, waxed jacket and Peter Storm overtrousers and matching seamless waterproof top coat. The latter is really superb, and I thoroughly recommend it as foulweather clothing. Worn over the waxed jacket, it ensures that not one drop of water gets through, and is worth every penny. As I stepped out of the van a gust of wind nearly bowled me over. I looked and felt like the Michelin man, but I knew that I would be warm and dry for the duration of the session.

After a short walk down Mad Moreton's private road, I arrived at the point swim, which I did not fancy one little bit. It looked dismal, with angry boils and heavy turbulence. The fact that my fishing position would have entailed driving rain hitting my face almost horizontally also helped in my decision to bypass the point at this stage of the proceedings. I could always return when the wind and rain had eased off, but for the time being the copse and bend swims would allow me to position myself with the elements at my back.

All right, so what if I am getting soft in my old age?

The inside run on the bend looked good, with five feet of steady water at that point, the main push of water being in mid-river and along the far bank. The prebaiting had been concentrated six yards downstream and three feet from the marginal rushes, and this is where I manoeuvred my meatpaste hookbait, by simply lowering it at my feet and allowing it to roll downstream with the current until the 1oz bomb hit bottom. The bail arm of the Cardinal 54 clicked over, and I was ready for action. I soon found that it was necessary to hold my rod low to the water to minimize the effects of the heavy, gusting wind on the quivertip, but even so the Betalight danced merrily in the darkness. I wondered if the 9lb 14oz fish I had landed the previous week from the same swim was still in residence. If so, with the favourable feeding conditions, it could now weigh well over ten pounds.

The quivertip slowly bending round

A Wensum twelve-pounder.

brought me back to the job in hand, but I did not strike. I knew it was not a bite. A massive pile of decaying weed, washed downstream by the floodwater, had fouled the line. I realized that the river was rising fast; the torrential rain was obviously running straight off the land and bringing the level up very quickly. Six more inches and the Wensum would burst its banks and be about two miles wide.

For the fourth time in as many minutes rubbish was cleared from the line, and then I made the decision to change the bomb from 1oz to ½oz, to allow the bait to roll round to fish tight against the marginal rushes. The first cast with this modified rig at least allowed me to fish a static bait for about five minutes, ample time for a barbel to home in on the smell of the meat. The

wind and rain continued unabated, and had I known what was still in store for me I would have realized that what I had so far experienced was but a gentle breeze.

The line tension on my finger suddenly relaxed a little, to be followed by the quivertip dipping as the tension returned and increased. The slow pull was unmissable, and the rod arced over as the hook went home. The clutch on my Abu 54 sang out as the fish kited into midstream, and soon the first barbel was being weighed at 7lb exactly. The split tail and two warts at the vent told me that it was a fish of 6lb 10oz I had caught the previous August. A seven-pound fish was a nice start to my week's holiday, and after depositing another six droppers of hemp into the swim I moved up into the copse.

The Wensum about to burst its banks.

When I arrived there the rain had eased a little and the brief appearance of the moon through the black clouds allowed me a good look at the swim in the strong moonlight. The crease in the swim was clearly visible, the far-bank boils and surface turbulence being replaced by a much steadier, though still very fast flow in mid-river. Again, the near bank provided the best option under the conditions that prevailed; with an evenly paced smooth glide it looked the perfect swim. Once more the moon disappeared, the rain returned and sheets of water were again propelled along the Wensum valley by the howling gale.

The 1oz lead hit bottom just past mid-river, bounced twice and then held. The stinging rain in my face soon convinced me that my normal upstream presentation would have to be abandoned in favour of a downstream leger approach, where I could sit with the wind at my back. I told you I was getting soft. Out went the lead again, and it rolled round to settle about two yards from the near bank. The rod was pointed directly at the bait, the line held under tension in my left hand. Seconds later there was a nudge on my fingers, but no pull followed. You crafty so and so, I thought, as I realized that I had just missed a possible second barbel. Moving the bait a couple of times failed to elicit any further response from the culprit, and so I recast. Instantly there were two more nudges and a pull, but my strike met with no resistance whatever. The barbel were obviously feeding over the hemp but appeared very nervy, so I decided to give them six more bait droppers of the seed before leaving them to gain more confidence. After all, they were not going anywhere, and I had all night.

The point swim looked hopeless. The two converging flows joined in a twisting, boiling cauldron of brown, turbid floodwater. It was impossible to hold upstream by the far-bank bushes in this volume of water, and I soon abandoned the attempt. The river had risen over two inches since I had prebaited the swim in the afternoon. I realized that it was now unfishable and getting worse.

Half an hour back in the bottom bend produced a horrible little eel, after I had eventually connected with the third bite from the slimy creature, and then it was time to move back to the copse. A meat-paste bait was lowered directly on top of the hemp pile and in seconds I felt a sharp rap on my finger. A firm lift of the rod resulted in the rod hooping over most impressively. This was no eel. I eased off the pressure as the line cut upstream through the water, and then the rod top thumped as the barbel held position in midstream. I knew it was a good fish and was now oblivious to the lashing rain in my face as the line sang in the strong wind. The barbel moved further upstream, in the direction of a mid-river snag that I had lost fish on before, and I piled on the pressure. The rod bent nearly double before the pressure told, and then the fish suddenly came up off the bottom, turned out into the main flow and belted off downstream at an alarming speed, assisted by a Wensum in full spate. The sheer power of that irresistible surge ensured that my addiction to barbel will last a lifetime.

I set off in pursuit and, when I was below the fish, made it work back upstream against the flow. My arm now felt as though it was about to drop off but I still had not made any significant impression on the barbel. Before long, however, it was under the rod top on a short line, still sulking deep, and, at about the seventh attempt to bring the fish to the surface, it eventually succumbed and sank into the waiting net. The torch beam soon revealed an absolutely belting fish of 9lb 14oz, perfect in fin and scale formation.

After the rigours of the fight, it was

necessary to hold her in a steady flow for about twenty minutes before a strong flip of her tail convinced me that she was fit enough to be returned to her home in the murky Wensum. A glance at my watch confirmed that it was now nearly half past one in the morning. A cup of hot tea and warm sleeping-bag seemed next on the agenda. After piling in the remainder of my bait, I made my way back to the van. The barbel would still be there tomorrow and perhaps the wind and rain would have blown over.

I awoke at 9 a.m. and by the time I had washed, shaved and enjoyed a leisurely breakfast, helped down by half a gallon of tea, it was nearly midday. The sun was shining as I strolled down to the river, and I remember thinking that one more teaspoon of water would see the Wensum spewing all over the fields. Another two inches had gone in since I had packed up just a few hours earlier.

Fifteen bait droppers of hemp went into both the steady runs of the copse and bend swims. The river really was moving like an express train that morning, and it was obvious that all the weir gates along the whole length of the Wensum valley were now wide open. I smiled at the thought that there would probably be a water shortage in Norfolk in July. In an hour, the level had dropped six inches, the water-borne rubbish problem diminishing as the level receded. Conditions now looked perfect and my confidence in further barbel action was sky-high.

I was in no hurry to start fishing, for I intended to fish all the dark hours that night, and in early afternoon I fed the swims again, a dozen droppers in each. The wind was getting up again and ominous black clouds scuttled overhead. Soon the rain started, a light drizzle at first but steadily becoming heavier with each squall of wind.

The lead held in mid-river and then suddenly moved downstream, creating slack line. The strike met with a solid response and the clutch buzzed as the barbel moved for the far-bank tree roots. Soon the scales were recording two ounces under six pounds. On the next cast, the lead bounced twice from the holding position, as a result of the attentions of a 6½-pounder, and then it was time to head back to the van for my evening meal. After that the serious business of the after-dark session would begin.

As I waited impatiently for the delicious beef stew that was boiling enticingly on the stove, the rain hammered on the roof with such power that it sounded like a whole herd of tap-dancing frogs. Once more the wind howled, its speed increasing with every minute that passed, and the ominous roars of thunder in the distance warned me that what I was now experiencing was merely a dress rehearsal for the real thing. After my meal, a loud cracking of a willow branch about twenty yards from the van startled me out of the forty winks I was just enjoying before heading back down to the river, and at the same instant a deafening crash of thunder erupted and a blinding flash of lightning illuminated the scene. Tonight's session promised to be wet and wild. I didn't know the half of it.

After putting on the wet-weather gear again I set off into the Norfolk night. I was just climbing the fence at the end of Mad Moreton's drive when an explosion of thunder directly overhead and a burning spear of lightning that seemed to head directly at me sent me half jumping and half falling off the gate. In an effort to avoid frying, I threw the carbon rod away from me, into the field. Less than three hundred yards away, there was a deafening crack as the big old ivy-covered tree at the bend was struck down. At almost the same instant there was another almighty crash behind me, and I turned to see another tree crumpling across the pathway I had walked only minutes earlier. The crescendo of noise rose to awe-inspiring proportions as I slowly made my way to the copse swim, and my mind was filled with the conflicting emotions of fear and excitement. Never before had I witnessed nature in such an angry mood.

As I neared the swim a broken tree branch smashed into my back as I temporarily halted its mad dash across the storm-lashed fields, for all the world like tumbleweed in a western movie. Heavier and heavier the rain beat down, and the rolls of thunder and flashes of lightning became more and more frequent until the countryside was a scene of pure primitive bedlam.

Once in position at the copse swim, I tied the umbrella cords to two bank sticks pushed two feet into the soft earth, and then positioned the pole so that the umbrella would be at as low an angle as possible. How I erected the brolly without losing it I do not know, but eventually I was sheltering under the protection it afforded, with the stays creaking and groaning under the onslaught of the gale. The noise under the umbrella was fantastic, and I felt that at any moment the green fabric would be torn away from the ribs. As the lightning lit up the night sky like a Guy Fawkes display, I knew that I must be mad to be fishing under such conditions.

For two hours I sat out the full force of that hurricane, the elements that night destroying everything in their path. Before my eyes, I could see the river rising once more, and within thirty minutes it had reached the top of the bank. Soon the Wensum could hold no more water, and raging floodwater spilled over into the fields. Fascinated, I watched the birth of a new river, which deserted the original path to the bottom bend but raced directly across the grass towards the railway bridge. Thousands of gallons of water poured through that breach, and before long I was surrounded by water, six inches up my tackle box and still rising steadily. The wind force intensified still further, and then one of the umbrella stays snapped, the fabric slamming into my cheek. I hung on to the brolly pole for grim death as a steadily deepening Wensum raged all around me.

The few brain cells that dish out my common sense were urging me to quit while there was still time and head back to the comparative safety of the van. As I contemplated the raging hurricane I laughed out loud as I recalled the words of Michael Fish on television 'The weather will probably get worse before it gets better,' he had said. Was he right, or what?

Just then a massive barbel rolled over the baited area, the second big fish I'd seen in an hour. If only the wind and rain would ease, to enable me to lift the brolly a little, I felt sure that barbel would be mine. Slowly the hurricane moved eastwards, the thunder sounding like the distant booming of artillery. Although the rain continued unabated and the lightning continued to illuminate my watery surroundings, the wind dropped enough to allow me to reposition the umbrella so that I could fish in reasonable comfort. What a night! I felt totally exhilarated by the whole experience.

The meat paste plopped into mid-river, upstream of the baited area, before the flow picked up the line, pushing it downstream so that the bait settled three yards below the breach in the bank. Immediately, the quivertip wrenched round, and the resulting strike saw the hook take a solid hold in barbel flesh. I cracked my head on the umbrella pole in my attempt to escape its confines. As I often experienced before with big barbel, the fish stayed deep and unmoving, swaying from side to side in the heavy flow. Once I had got below it, with the wind and rain lashing into my face and the line making tinny noises, the fish was encouraged to move back upstream. As I sensed it was approaching that dangerous snag, easing the pressure somewhat had the effect of making the barbel stop its fight against the restriction, and it once again merely held its station. Gently, I eased it back downstream towards me, and then again increased pressure enough to startle the barbel into fighting back and make it battle its way back against the flow once more. Four times this manoeuvre was repeated, tiring the barbel all the time, and I could feel that the fish was steadily becoming higher in the water. Eventually she broke surface and after a couple of swirls she was mine. Immediately, I could see that she was indeed a massive fish, and one that I recognized straight away. Because of that, I knew approximately what she would weigh, and I soon recorded a weight of 12lb 10oz, 2oz lighter than when I had caught her to record my personal best barbel. This brilliant fish would ensure that the night of the hurricane was one that I would never forget.

After sacking up the twelve-pounder in the field, away from the heavy flow of the main river, I smoked two cigarettes in quick succession while I basked in a glow of satisfaction. Soon I was fishing again, and the very next cast saw the lead move, to be followed by the hiss of the clutch as ten yards of line whistled off the spool. After that initial surge the fight was quite

Beau – the queen of the Wensum.

short-lived, with the fish swimming straight into the net. Six pounds fourteen ounces that barbel weighed, and she went back strongly after being held for about ten minutes.

Just after I had checked the big fish in the sack, a whole tree came floating past, its massive roots pointing dejectedly towards the sky, while the ferocious rain continued unabated. Tomorrow I doubted whether I would be able to get anywhere near the river, let alone be able to fish.

After resuming fishing I sat for twenty biteless minutes before deciding to twitch the bait. Immediately, a strong wrench followed, and seconds later a big fish had powered out to midstream and was belting off down river. I was now surrounded by water and had no idea of where the original bank was located, and it was obviously dangerous to try to follow the fish downstream. I would have to play it from the position where I had hooked it.

Slowly, I pumped the fish back upstream until it was level with me, when I felt once more in control. Suddenly a tree branch hurtling downstream picked up the line before I had chance to take any evasive action. I heaved for all I was worth to free the tackle, succeeding in drawing the barbel up amongst the tangle of branches, before the timber floated away downstream. I heard the barbel thrash at the surface and then the line fell slack. The hooklink had broken just above the hook. Although I felt sick that I had left a hook in a fish, I had the consolation that there was not a trailing length of line to worry about. Losing that barbel was down to the elements and sheer bad luck.

After I had sorted out the gear and recast, I did not have long to wait before the rod once more pulled over in a three-foot lunge. Again, a big barbel hugged the bottom and moved slowly upstream. A repeat of my previous technique with the twelve-

pounder again proved successful, and I was soon removing my size 4 Au Lion d'Or from a 9lb 9oz meat gobbler.

That was the end of the action for that night, and after releasing the twelve-pounder I headed back to the van absolutely shattered – but on cloud nine. What a truly remarkable eight hours! The combination of driving rain, hurricane-force wind, lightning and deafening thunder meant that I had experienced the emotions of fear, excitement, anger, frustration, elation and total satisfaction. That night of the hurricane I will remember for the rest of my life. It was a totally exhilarating experience.

The persistent rain bouncing on the van roof prevented sleep for what seemed an eternity, but I eventually awoke to the sound of chainsaws. The sight that met my eyes as I stepped out of the van was unbelievable. Total devastation was everywhere, with telephone lines down, trees uprooted, branches scattered around, slates off the cottage roofs and the road blocked by dozens of toppled trees. It was as if World War Three had hit Norfolk in the night.

The news reports of the effects of the hurricane nation-wide were frightening, with forty-four people killed and hundreds injured. Norfolk was cut off for days, with roads impassable, and electricity and phone supplies disrupted. There was worse to come. The Wensum was, in places, five miles wide. It was obviously unfishable, and all day I helped the Shortis family clear up the heart-breaking destruction that had been wrought on the estate. The extent of the damage was colossal, and when I thought that I had actually sat out and fished all night through the worst storm to hit this country in living memory I realized that I must have been stupid. On reflection, I was risking my own life as well as the future of my wife and daughters, but still say that I would not have missed the experience for anything.

An hour before dark, I baited a swim at the edge of the weir pool, where there was smooth water well away from the raging torrent in mid-river. I really fancied that for a barbel bite but really it was Hobson's choice. Nowhere else on the river was fishable anyway. An hour after dark I was settled in and a good chub of 4¼lb rewarded my second cast. That was a welcome confidence booster. If a chub could find the bait so could a barbel, and I fished on with renewed enthusiasm.

A short while later a strike at a lead movement connected with nothing, but I was still convinced that there was a barbel to be caught in the pool that night. I had one of those unshakeable convictions, a feeling that I have learned never to ignore. An hour later a firm pluck and pull justified my faith, and the hook connected with a big chunk of barbel. Ten minutes later I still had not moved the fish off the bottom and I began to wonder if I had at last set my hook in the mammoth barbel that Dave Plummer and I had first seen three years previously, which we had christened Split-O, on account of the neat split in its huge dorsal, which makes the fin appear to hang either side of its body. We originally estimated the fish at about fourteen pounds, and Dave actually hooked it twice. That wily old beast had, however, managed to escape both times. With this in mind, my excitement was rising.

Slowly the barbel came up off the bottom and hung in midwater, defying the full force of the Wensum flood. I got the merest glimpse of the fish before she went deep again, and knew that she was big – very big. Walking down to the bush that grows out from the weir wall, I was able to ease the huge fish into the slacker water and draw her into the waiting net 'Got you, you belter,' I shouted out loud, and then my heart

was pounding and my hands shaking as I recognized that unmistakable split dorsal. Scarcely daring to breathe, I placed that magnificent barbel into the weigh bag for the moment of truth.

I knew that the barbel was big, but I also knew that she lacked the solidness of some of the other very big barbel that Dave and I had caught over the years. This made her look a lot bigger in the water than she actually was. Three years previously she may well have established a new barbel record, but she was not of those proportions now. The scales confirmed an immense 12lb 12oz, equalling my personal best barbel. At that moment I knew that my affair with the Wensum barbel was probably drawing to a close. I had caught the barbel that had figured in so many of my dreams, and had now had the two largest barbel known to inhabit that particular section of river pick up my baits on successive nights. In less than twenty-four hours I had taken two twelve-pounders from an inhospitable, raging Wensum, and I was a very contented barbel angler.

Having landed Split-O, I knew that this would be my last season on the Wensum, and I would now be looking for pastures new. The Bristol Avon would next receive my attention. With these thoughts going through my mind, I returned to the van, climbed into the sleeping bag, and slept for fourteen hours solid.

While I slept the river dropped a foot and access to the bottom field was again possible. Standing in two feet of water beside the copse, I soon landed barbel of 5lb 14oz, 6lb 8oz and 7lb 2oz, as well as seeing another double-figure fish throw the hook at the rim of the landing net. After the success I had already enjoyed, I was able to smile. You can't win them all.

After dark, I caught the smallest barbel I had ever landed from the Wensum, at 1lb 14oz. That fish nearly died on me, taking a

Dave Plummer with a fabulous Wensum fish of 13lb 6oz.

good hour to recover before I dared release it. It eventually darted away – much to my relief. That small fish pleased me no end, as it represented a true home-grown barbel, possibly a twelve-pounder of the future.

The following morning I made my slow way home, physically exhausted but mentally satisfied with the few days' hurricane barbel fishing I had experienced. After sorting out a few minor problems, I was back on the Wensum two days later for my final fling on this lovely barbel river. The river had dropped a foot since my departure but retained some colour. Conditions looked absolutely dead-on, and once more I baited the copse, the point and the bottom bend. I hoped to catch a barbel from each swim, as a kind of farewell gesture to the countless happy hours I had spent in each of them.

The bottom bend produced a 9½-pounder that fought like the devil before it allowed me to draw it into the landing net. The point, scene of so many triumphs, bade farewell with a chunky fish of 5lb 14oz. The copse had a last surprise for me. The meat bounced down the crease in mid-river, held for a minute, and then the line fell slack. The strike was successful, and immediately I knew that I had hooked another big fish. Once again the barbel initially hung in mid-river, just swaying in the current and refusing to be budged. After

Beau again and our last goodbye when she weighed 12lb 2oz.

that, the fish came into the net quite easily, and as she did so a wry smile came to my lips. Here was an old friend, obviously come to say goodbye. The scales said 12lb 2oz, the fish being the same one that I had landed at 12lb 10oz on the night of the hurricane.

As I slipped her back, I reminisced over what a lovely friend she has been to me ever since she became my first ever double, and still my equal personal best. I have watched her for hours, and learned a lot about barbel behaviour from my observations. If a fish could be knighted for services to anglers, then Beau, as she is called, must surely be near the head of the queue. The pleasure and excitement she has given to me and to countless other anglers makes her truly a princess amongst barbel.

To sum up, then. In just seven days' fishing, fifteen barbel came to net for a total weight of about 120lb, an average of 8lb. Three twelve-pounders had made it a memorable occasion, even if I had to sit through the teeth of a very dramatic hurricane to do it. I had enjoyed every minute. That hurricane barbel fishing was certainly the wettest, windiest, wildest and most wonderful Wensum week Westy ever had!

Conclusion

We all derive our pleasure from barbel angling in different ways. In this book you have read our thoughts and approaches to fishing for this most exciting fish of flowing water. Nothing has been held back, and we can only hope that you go on to gain as much pleasure and excitement from barbel fishing as we do.

We do not expect you to agree with everything we have said. In fact, we would be surprised if you did. After all, constructive debate and argument is the way in which we all increase our knowledge. We only ask that you give our methods a fair trial. We are confident that you will have no cause to regret it.

The pleasure we have enjoyed in our barbel angling has been greatly enhanced by the fact that most of the men who share our addiction are thoroughly amiable people. We can only, therefore, end this book as we began, by thanking all those whose friendship has contributed to our immense store of happy memories.

We must never lose sight of the fact that fishing should be for fun. Ambition to catch bigger and bigger fish should never be allowed to dominate your life to such extent that it becomes a life-or-death crusade. If you reach that point, you have forgotten the reason for going fishing in the first place.

For this reason, we have tried to emphasize the importance we place on humour. As well as the serious business of catching big fish, there should always be time for a laugh. We would end with our adaptation of the famous saying that fishing consists of a fool at one end and a worm at the other. For really enjoyable barbel angling, there should be a jerk at both ends!

Index

INDEX

Other fishing books published by The Crowood Press